M000098327

Early European Drama in Translation

# MEDIEVAL DUTCH DRAMA

## FOUR SECULAR PLAYS AND FOUR FARCES
## FROM THE VAN HULTHEM MANUSCRIPT

Translated with an Introduction by
### Johanna C. Prins

© Copyright 1999
Pegasus Press
Asheville, North Carolina

LIBRARY OF CONGRESS CATALOGING-IN-PUBLICATIONS DATA

Medieval Dutch drama : four secular plays and four farces from the Van Hulthem
manuscript / translated with an introduction by Johanna C. Prins.
    p.   cm.—(Early European drama translation series ; 3)
Includes bibliographical references.
ISBN 1-889818-07-0 (alk. paper)
    I. Dutch drama—To 1500—Translations, English.  I. Prins, Johanna C., 1934–
II. Series.

PT5495.E5 M43  1999
839.3'1208001—dc21

                                                            99-045763

This book is made to last.
It is printed on acid-free paper
to library specifications.

Printed in the United States of America

# Early European Drama in Translation Series

MARTIN STEVENS, FOUNDING EDITOR
STEPHEN K. WRIGHT, GENERAL EDITOR

# MEDIEVAL DUTCH DRAMA

FOUR SECULAR PLAYS AND FOUR FARCES
FROM THE VAN HULTHEM MANUSCRIPT

Translated with an Introduction by
Johanna C. Prins

The
# 𝔈arly 𝔈uropean 𝔇rama in 𝔗ranslation
## Series

The Early European Drama Translation Series is a project established under the auspices of the Medieval and Renaissance Drama Society. The purpose of the EEDT series is to provide reliable, inexpensive translations of major European vernacular plays from the Middle Ages and Renaissance for use in a wide variety of undergraduate and graduate courses. It is the explicit intent of the series to internationalize the teaching and study of the early theater by supplying translations of important texts from many genres: mystery plays, saint plays, history plays, miracles, moralities, folk plays, carnival plays, processionals, and civic and ecclesiastical ceremonies of every kind.

Martin Stevens and Stephen K. Wright are the Founding Editor and General Editor of the EEDT series, respectively. Members of the Advisory Board include Kathleen Ashley, Konrad Eisenbichler, Kathleen Falvey, Gordon Kipling, Alan E. Knight, Robert Potter, and Eckehard Simon.

Volume One: Arnoul Gréban: *The Mystery of the Passion, The Third Day*, translated by Paula Giuliano

Volume Two: *Antichrist and Judgment Day: The Middle French "Jour du Jugement,"* translated by Richard K. Emmerson and David F. Hult

Volume Three: *Medieval Dutch Drama: Four Secular Plays and Four Farces from the Van Hulthem Manuscript*, translated by Johanna C. Prins

# CONTENTS

Acknowledgments      vi

Introduction      vii

The Manuscript      vii
     Publication History      ix
     Literary Relations      xi
     Language      xiv
     Style and Structure      xv
     Performance      xvii
     Criticism      xix
     Individual Plays and Farces      xxiv

The Translation      xxxv
     Notes      xxxvii
     Part One: *Esmoreit* and *Lippin*      I
     Part Two: *Gloriant* and *Blow-in-the-Box*      55
     Part Three: *Lancelot of Denmark* and *The Witch*      113
     Part Four: *Debate of Winter and Summer* and *Ruben*      157

Appendix: Facsimile and Transcription      197

Bibliography      201

# Acknowledgments

My work on the Dutch *abel* plays and farces translated in this book began during the NEH Summer Seminar "Shakespeare and the Native Dramatic Tradition" directed by Professor Martin Stevens at Columbia University in 1991. I am grateful to the National Endowment for the Humanities for enabling me to attend the Seminar, and to Professor Stevens and the other members of the Seminar for many stimulating discussions. Professor Stevens encouraged this project from the beginning and guided early versions of the work.

Several friends have read parts of the manuscript and given valuable advice on substance and style. Sylvia Tomasch read and helped me organize the Introduction. Mary-Jo Arn, Ken Heimrich, and Diane Marks read individual plays and made many suggestions for improvements in the translations. Professor Peter Beidler used an early version of *Lancelot of Denmark* in a course in Medieval Drama at Baylor University and provided many helpful comments and questions from his students. From the Netherlands, Dieuwke van der Poel and Frank Meurs sent suggestions for critical material as well as their own work on the plays, and Professor Herman Pleij, Professor Hans van Dijk, and Bart Besamusca also sent material not available to me in New York. I felt enormously supported by this transcontinental network and I thank everyone for their support. Finally, Professor Stephen K. Wright read the completed manuscript and made many helpful suggestions. I owe a great debt to all these friends and colleagues, without whom this project would have been much more difficult. Naturally, the responsibility for the finished product is all mine.

Johanna C. Prins
1999

# INTRODUCTION

## THE MANUSCRIPT

The Van Hulthem Manuscript, which contains the plays translated in this volume, is named for the Ghent magistrate Charles Van Hulthem who bought it at auction in 1811. Van Hulthem himself noted on the inside of the front cover that it came from the library of a certain A. J. Nuewens in Brussels.[1] The provenance before this date is unknown. After Van Hulthem's death in 1832 his entire library, including this manuscript, was purchased by the State of Belgium. His collection became the foundation for the Royal Library in Brussels, where the Van Hulthem Manuscript itself still resides.[2] The signature of the Van Hulthem Manuscript is 15.589–623.[3]

The early fifteenth-century manuscript is not a showpiece. It is the work of a single copyist who transcribed his texts on paper, in two columns and with virtually no decoration. In addition to the rubrics, small capitals at the beginning of a text appear throughout the manuscript in red ink, which is also used to draw cross-strokes through the initial letter of each line (separated from the rest of the line by a space). Individual texts are numbered in red ink as well. The use of the *littera cursiva*, which is faster and more economical than the more formal *littera textualis* typically used for literary or religious works, suggests that the book was not made for a wealthy collector.[4] The 241 folios contain 214 different numbered pieces of various kinds: fragments of Jacob van Maerlant's *Spieghel Historiael* (an adaptation of Vincent of Beauvais' *Speculum Historiale*) and the *Historie van Troyen* (*History of Troy*), the Middle Dutch version of *La Châtelaine de Vergi*, *The Miracle of Theophilus*, and many other works. In fact, the collection is so varied that scholars have wondered how or why these pieces were brought together in one volume.

One hypothesis is that the manuscript belonged to a copyist's workshop, where customers could select texts that they wanted to have copied. That would explain why the number of lines of each piece appears at the end, because the copyist was paid by the line. Another possibility is that texts or plays could be custom-ordered from samples in the manuscript, a practice similar to what has been observed about painting studios.[5] This explanation might account for one short text in the manuscript, "A Beginning for All Plays" (*Een beginsel van allen spelen*, number 207, 52 lines), an all-purpose prologue suitable for any play.

Among the contents of the manuscript, four plays called "*abel* plays" (usually translated as 'handsome,' 'ingenious,' or 'serious' plays), *Esmoreit, Gloriant, Lancelot of Denmark*, and *The Debate of Winter and Summer*, and the farces following each of them have drawn a great deal of attention from scholars of medieval drama because of their unique characteristics. The *abel* plays are serious, secular plays from the fourteenth century, each of which is followed by a farce. The full rubric of the first is: "An *abel* play of Esmoreit, son of the king of Sicily, and a farce following it" ('*Een abel spel van esmoreit / tconincx sone van cecielien ende ene / sotternie daer na volghende*').[6] This play is called *Esmoreit* and the farce *Lippin*. For the second play the rubric reads: "An *abel* play and noble tale of the Duke of Brunswick and how he fell in love with the daughter of the Red Lion of Abelant and a farce following it" ('*Een abel spel ende een edel dinc / vanden hertoghe van bru-uyswijc / hoe hi wert minnende des roede / lioens dochter van abelant / Ende ene sotternie na volgende*'). This play is *Gloriant*, named after the Duke of Brunswick; the farce is called *Blow-in-the-Box* (*Buskenblaser*). The third play, here called *Lancelot of Denmark*, is "An *abel* play of Lancelot of Denmark how he fell in love with a maiden who served his mother and a farce following it" ('*Een abel spel van lanseloet van / denemerken hoe hi wert minnende / ene joncfrouwe die met sijnder moerder / diende. Ende ene sotternie na volghende*').[7] The farce is called *The Witch* ('Die Hexe'). Finally, there is "An *abel* play of the winter and the summer and a farce following it" ('*Een abel spel vanden winter / Ende vanden somer. Ende ene / Sotternie na volghende*'), here called *The Debate of Winter and Summer*; the accompanying farce is called *Ruben*.

The plays are not strictly grouped together in the manuscript. *Esmoreit* and *Lippin* are numbered 169 and 170, *Gloriant* and *Blow-in-the-Box* are numbered together as 205, *Lancelot of Denmark* and *The Witch* are number 206, and *The Debate of Winter and Summer* and *Ruben* are number 211. But they are often treated together because of their common characteristics and because they are all identified in the manuscript as *abele spelen,* "abel plays."[8] Each of the plays is announced in the rubric as *"een abel spel van . . . ene sotternie na volgende,"* that is to say, "an abel play of . . . and a farce following."[9] The adjective *abel* or *abele* (depending on grammatical context) has provoked considerable discussion, since the word is rare in Middle Dutch and the meaning is not entirely clear. Of the citations under *abel* in the *Middle Dutch Dictionary,* about one third are from the *abel* plays, and the translations are clearly determined by the editors' interpretations of the genre of those plays. Two other texts in the manuscript have *abel* in their rubric, such as "An *abel* tale of Our Lady," but these do not add anything to our understanding. Cognate with Latin *habilis,* German *hablich* or *häblich*[10] and English *able,* the word has been translated as 'fit,' 'expert,' 'handsome,' 'ingenious,' 'serious,' or 'artful,' always in reference to the plays, and is sometimes taken as an indication of their genre. Whatever *abel* may mean, these are serious, secular plays; that is to say, they are not farces, though they contain many touches of humor, and while their subject matter is not primarily religious, they are steeped in religious sentiment and conviction.

While the dialect of the scribe cannot be localized precisely (see below under Language), various texts in the manuscript can be connected to Brussels: a report of a miracle that took place in Brussels in September 1399, very shortly before the manuscript was composed, for instance.[11] In fact, the very range and variety of the contents suggests a connection with a fairly large town. Examination of the watermarks indicates that the manuscript must have been composed between 1400 and 1410. Repair work performed circa 1550–1570 indicates that the volume had already seen heavy use by that time.[12]

## Publication History

Only one of the *abel* plays from the Van Hulthem manuscript made its way into print at an early date. An incunabular edition of the play of

*Lancelot* was issued in Gouda circa 1486. Unfortunately, the unique extant copy of this edition was lost during World War II.[13] Two later editions were printed in the first quarter of the sixteenth century and several more in the seventeenth century. Two separate German translations appeared circa 1500, testifying to the widespread popularity of this play.[14] The title pages of the incunabular and the post-incunabular editions describe the play as a *Historie* rather than a *Spel*, indicating that it was seen primarily as a reading text rather than a performable play. One of the later editions adds that the text is "*Ghenoechlike . . . om te lesen*," that is, "pleasant to read." It is therefore interesting to note that the recent discovery of two paper rolls containing the parts of the two major characters, dating from around 1700, shows that *Lancelot* was still being acted at that late date.[15]

The attention of modern scholars was first drawn to the *abel* plays by C. P. Serrure, who published a French translation of *Esmoreit, Le Jeu d'Esmorée, Fils du Roi de Sicile, Drame flamand du XIIIe siècle*, in 1828.[16] After editions of the medieval Dutch text were published by H. Hoffmann von Fallersleben in 1838 and H. E. Moltzer in 1868–75, P. Leendertz, Jr. brought out the standard edition in his *Middelnederlandsche dramatische poëzie* (Leiden, 1907). A more recent one-volume diplomatic edition of all four *abel* plays with the appended farces was published by Louise van Kammen in 1968; this edition is the basis for the present translation.[17] Among the numerous and excellent school editions of individual plays, those published by R. Roemans and R. Gaspard (*Esmoreit* and *Gloriant*), by Roemans and H. van Assche (*Lancelot of Denmark*), and by G. Stellinga (*The Debate of Winter and Summer*) are useful to the scholar because of their extensive bibliographies.

*Esmoreit* was translated into English by H. M. Ayres in 1924 and by J. Oakshott and E. Strietman in 1986. *Lancelot* was translated into English by P. Geyl and also by E. Colledge. *Lippin, Blow-in-the-Box*, and *Ruben* have been translated by Therese Decker and Martin Walsh.[18]

## Literary Relations

The surviving corpus of medieval theater texts, especially in England, is dominated by religious drama. David Bevington's classic anthology *Medieval Drama* (1975) includes no secular drama dating from before the sixteenth century. More recently, C. Clifford Flanigan's overview "Comparative Literature and the Study of Medieval Drama" (1986) refers to secular drama and the *abel* plays a few times, but does not discuss them at length.[19] Most records from the Low Countries also refer only to religious plays, but the artistic quality of the *abel* plays in the Van Hulthem manuscript makes it unlikely that they were the only secular plays of their time.[20] Only recently have attempts been made to integrate studies of medieval drama internationally, as exemplified by the collection of articles edited by Eckehard Simon in *The Theater of Medieval Europe* (1991).[21] Few secular plays from before circa 1400 survive, and scholars have found no direct precursors for the *abel* plays.

Yet even if the *abel* plays were unique for their time, they still have much in common with other European literatures of the Middle Ages. One of these shared elements is the depiction of *fin'amor*, the love that elevates and ennobles the lovers; that puts the beloved lady on a pedestal (though not necessarily after marriage); the love that is an inescapable force, striking its "victims" with overwhelming suddenness and then controlling their hearts and minds; the love that is threatened by evil outsiders, the spies and tellers of lies, such as Florentine's jealous cousin in *Gloriant*. Although in recent years both the meaning and the importance of *fin'amor* have been questioned from many angles,[22] and while the *abel* plays are by no means consistent in their presentation of courtly ideology, they do show traces of its language, such as the emphatic rejection of *dorpernie* (French *vileinie*), which is the opposite of courtliness.[23] Whatever *fin'amor* may have meant in the twelfth century when Andreas Capellanus wrote his famous treatise on love, its meaning would have changed considerably by 1400. Furthermore, because it is difficult to be certain about the audience for the *abel* plays, it is also difficult, if not impossible, to ascertain their interest in and attitude towards such matters. Court or town records make no mention of these specific plays; references to plays in general are extremely infrequent, so sparse that it is easy to make too much of them. One can safely say only that, while entertainers of various kinds came to the courts, *plays* were mostly performed in the towns and that the nobles went to see them there.[24]

Herman Pleij has pointed out that the combination of *abel* plays and farces seems particularly suitable to the interests and aspirations of the bourgeoisie in the towns.[25] As towns became more important and powerful in the Low Countries (and Pleij sees this happening in the late fourteenth century), various groups of inhabitants started to express their ideas about the most desirable forms of personal and social behavior, in the relations between men and women for instance. The town of Brussels, with which the Van Hulthem manuscript is linked, is estimated to have had as many as 40,000 inhabitants in the fourteenth century.[26] In such a town the literary life would have been varied, but the inhabitants would have been likely to agree in defining themselves in contrast to, for instance, the peasants, who are often the object of satire in the farces.

As towns expanded, marriage as an institution became subject to redefinition. The *abel* plays, with their idealized, vaguely courtly relationships between men and women, present one model in which class and gender relations appear to be somewhat fluid. The growing confidence of the bourgeoisie shows itself in the dismissal of class distinctions as an impediment to marriage (as in *Lancelot of Denmark*). The relationship between men and women presented in these plays allows room for initiative on the part of women (witness Damiet in *Esmoreit* and Florentine in *Gloriant*). In the farces, on the other hand, the picture is more conservative and the lessons are clear: beware of women who tyrannize their husbands, avoid "unequal marriages" between old men and young women, and guard against women who pursue their own sexual pleasure.[27] In this way, lessons about marriage are offered in the atmospheres of two very different social milieus: the noble circles of the King of Sicily or Duke of Brunswick in the *abel* plays and the peasant world in the farces. The space between these two milieus is precisely the same social space inhabited by the most likely audience for the plays, namely, the townspeople. Thus the need for privacy mentioned by other authors of the time is indirectly shown by its negative, the complete lack of privacy in the farces, where a neighbor may run into and out of another's house. Rather than being "jewels of popular life and art," the farces can be seen as "caricatures of peasants and laborers in contrast with the ideals of behavior by which the established bourgeoisie wanted to be distinguished."[28]

In addition to *fin'amor*, the *abel* plays also exhibit several other familiar elements found in the literature of various European countries, such as the motif of the accused queen. Together with Chaucer's Constance in the *Man of Law's Tale*, the queen in *Esmoreit* is the primary object of study in Margaret Schlauch's book on this topos.[29] The villain Robert, who suggests that the queen has committed adultery with a younger man, plays explicitly on the old king's anxiety about his young wife, a characteristic problem in tales of unequal marriage. Another common gendered motif is the conversion of a pagan princess for the sake of love. Both Damiet, in *Esmoreit*, and Florentine, in *Gloriant*, convert to Christianity for the sake of their lovers, as Guibour did in the French epic cycle of Guillaume d'Orange.[30]

Because these same motifs can also be found in the *Miracles de Nostre Dame par personnages*, some critics have seen a literary relation between these French works and the Dutch *abel* plays.[31] The forty miracle plays were presented annually by the Goldsmiths' Guild of Paris between 1339 and 1382 and draw their material from traditional Christian legend and the *chansons de geste*.[32] But as their title indicates, the *Miracles de Nostre Dame* are religious plays, in contrast with the purely secular subject matter of the *abel* plays. As is common in medieval literature, the Muslims in *Esmoreit* and *Gloriant* are portrayed schematically as "others," who swear by Mohammed, Tervagant, or Apollo, but have few other exotic qualities. Even in the pagan world, for instance, characters may tell time in Christian terms, as when Platus says he was watching the stars at the time of Matins (*Esmoreit*, 64). Just as incongruously, Florentine's cousin Floriant (in *Gloriant*) refers to his own world as "*heydenesse*," or 'pagandom' (715).

## Language

Within what is called "Middle Dutch" there are many regional variations. Moving from west to east in the area that is now northern Belgium, one can distinguish three major dialects: Flemish, the language of the county of Flanders that was used in the works of Jacob van Maerlant (thirteenth century); Brabant, the language of the duchy of Brabant that was used by the mystic Hadewijch in the thirteenth century and that was later the language of *Elckerlijc* (the Dutch version of *Everyman*); and Limburg, the language of the duchy of that name and of Heinric van Veldeke's *Sint Servaes* in the twelfth century. Yet the differences between these dialects are not always very great, and as a result critical opinion is divided on the question of whether the *abel* plays are written in Flemish or Brabant. According to Roemans and Van Assche's brief survey of the debate, scholars base their arguments variously on dialectal differences and on geographical references in the texts.[33] The connection of other texts in the Van Hulthem manuscript to Brussels is also invoked. Mention of the towns of Kortrijk and Ghent in *The Witch* (lines 47 and 51) seems to argue for Flanders as the home of the plays, although by this reasoning the naming of Maastricht in *The Debate of Winter and Summer* (line 623) should point to Limburg.

The differences in language between individual literary works are, of course, also influenced by other than geographical factors. The thirteenth-century *Roman van Walewein*, an Arthurian romance probably connected with the court of Flanders and written about a hundred years after Chrétien de Troyes composed his *Conte du Graal* for Count Philipe of Flanders, has far more words of French origin than do the *abel* plays.[34] This may be because the court of Flanders was generally bilingual or because the *Roman van Walewein* is a courtly work, influenced by French Arthurian romances. The *abel* plays, on the other hand, may contain fewer French words because they were written for a less noble, urban public. The few words of French origin in the plays stand out more because they are rarer, although the fact that some of them rhyme with words that are not French suggests that the French words were thoroughly integrated in the local language. Thus "creature" rhymes with "nature" or "figure," but also with Dutch *ure* ('hour'). On the other hand, some pairs of words of French origin usually occur together, such as *"proys"* ('noble,' 'loyal,' 'modest,' 'courageous,' 'lively,' from Old French *preux*) and *"gracyoys"* ('gracious'). This pair is used several times to describe Sandrine in *Lancelot of Denmark* and also in *Winter and Summer*. Since there seems to be a conscious pairing of terms, I have translated them with similar romance words. In *Gloriant*, *"proys"* is paired with *"oerghelyous"* (cf. Middle English *orguelous*, also of French origin) and clearly was meant to be favorable.

## Style and Structure

The four *abel* plays in the Van Hulthem manuscript and their accompanying farces are all written in the same verse form, namely, rhymed couplets. The lines are irregular in length, with four stresses and an indefinite number of unstressed syllables in every line. Typically, the rhyme straddles passages spoken by different characters, probably serving as a mnemonic device reminding the next speaker of his line. In the text of the two parts of *Sandrijn en Lanslot* (the two actors' parts of the seventeenth-century version of *Lancelot of Denmark*) the final word of the previous speaker is similarly given as a cue. The *Debate of Winter and Summer* is even linked by rhyme with the farce that follows it in the manuscript. Thus, the text flows continuously without stanzaic breaks. There are very few exceptions to this rule of the straddling cue rhyme, and closer study indicates that these exceptions are most likely either breaks in the action (with one character leaving the stage) or pauses in the spoken dialogue to allow for some physical by-play.[35] There are far more entrances and exits in passages that are linked by rhyme. Garmt Stuiveling's attempts to infer important breaks in the structure of the plays from the few exceptions to the cue rhyme seem rather exaggerated and are always based on modern stylistic values.[36] Stuiveling seeks to explain the rhyme breaks as structural markers, testifying to a mature compositional talent, but this attempt is not convincing, especially in the light of all we do not know about the fourteenth-century spectator.[37]

More persuasive is G. A. van Es' 1955 study of the treatment of time and distance in "*Het negeren van tijd en afstand in de Abele Spelen*" ('Disregarding Time and Distance in the *Abel* Plays'). Van Es discusses the frequent jumps from one geographical area to another (from Sicily to Damascus and back in *Esmoreit*, from Brunswick to "Abelant" and back in *Gloriant*), all places theoretically separated by vast distances and long journeys. Earlier critics had often attempted to alter the time-spans that seem implied in these journeys between two scenes, even assuming scene breaks in performance. Did the voyage from Sicily to Damascus take two weeks, two months, or two years? How young was the infant Esmoreit when he was abducted and how old was the princess Damiet when the infant was entrusted to her? These questions, Van Es argues, betray a literal-minded reading not justified by the text, which is often confused or vague about geography. In *Gloriant*, for example, the princess Florentine is said to be "*uten rijc / vanden stat van abelant*" ('from the realm of the city of Abelant,' lines 228–29), sometimes interpreted as Babylon or Babel, while her father's mother is from Antioch. In *Esmoreit*, the king of Damast (probably Damascus, but understood to be a country) lives in a town called Balderijs, said to be "*doer toerkien*" ('beyond Turkey,' lines 184–85 and 214–15). With such vague indications of place, the only thing that one can be sure of is that Damast and Abelant are far away in the pagan East.

The alternation of scenes in the Christian West with those in the pagan East, which as Van Es shows are ideological opposites rather than geographical entities, creates a binary structure in the plays. The action takes place at two locations that are in implicit contrast, and some of the characters move back and forth between these two locations with apparent disregard of distance and travel time.[38] Esmoreit is abducted from Sicily and brought to Damascus; when he hears from Damiet that he is a foundling, he goes back to Sicily to discover his parentage. Gloriant travels to "Abelant" to meet Florentine and declare his love to her; after some dangerous conflicts with Florentine's father they travel back to Brunswick to get married. These journeys, which might be assumed to take weeks or months, are accomplished during monologues varying from six to sixty lines, and the cue rhymes would suggest that these far-flung places were close to one another in an actual performance.

On the other hand, as Van Es has noted, liberties are also taken with the chronology, indicating a concern with composition rather than with realism.[39] Thus in *Esmoreit*, Platus buys the abducted infant from his evil uncle in Sicily and travels to Damascus (a journey that, in reality, as one critic notes, would have taken several months), where the child is entrusted to the princess Damiet. In the next scene, the queen in Sicily is accused of infanticide and thrown in jail. Rather than speculate about how long the journey to Damascus might have taken and at which moment the queen would have been accused, Van Es posits that the scenes are arranged in this order to create an opposition between scenes in the familiar sphere (Sicily) and those in the exotic East, even though this arrangement may violate the logical chronological order of events. The binary structure of the plays emphasizes the contrast between East and West or between pagan and Christian, even though some characters may try to ignore that contrast, as Gloriant seems to do. Places like Sicily or Brunswick represent noble courts in the Christian West rather than actual locations. In contrast, in *Lancelot of Denmark* there is no opposition between East and West, Christian or pagan. In fact, in Van Es' view there is no travel in that play except by characters of secondary importance—by everyone except Lancelot, that is.[40]

The fantastic geography in *Esmoreit* and *Gloriant* stands in contrast to the authentic place names in the farce *The Witch*, where the witch is said to be from Kortrijk (Courtrai, line 47) and to have been banished from Ghent (line 51). Both towns are in Flanders and are fairly near the area where the plays originated, so presumably both familiar to the audience. Perhaps this proximity would have made the satire even more biting. On a smaller scale, the binary structure seen in the *abel* plays also exists in the farces, where as Van Dijk notes the action alternates between scenes in the house and outdoors or between the familiar and the unconventional.[41]

## Performance

Stage directions in the plays of the Van Hulthem manuscript are rare and limited to basic instructions like "here they fight" ('*Hier vechtensi,' Lippin,* after line 184) or "here they hang Robert" (*'Robbrecht hanctmen hier,' Esmoreit* after line 995). But there can be little doubt that these texts are written to be performed. They are identified in the manuscript as "*spel,*" 'play,' in contrast to the later versions of *Lancelot,* which are called "*historie*" and "*ghenoechlike om te lesene,*" that is to say, a tale that is 'pleasant to read.'[42] The prologues and epilogues also point to a performance situation. The paucity of information available on the staging of the plays has led to a great deal of speculation, none of which can be verified. Both the *abel* plays and the farces are generally set in two different locations, and characters move from one location to another during extended monologues. This could best be accomplished by having two locations side by side on stage, but the manuscript gives no evidence of how this was done. Often, the action shifts from one location to another without a monologue. The difficulty in interpreting actors' movements in the plays is illustrated by a scene in the farce *Lippin,* which has the main character knocking at his own front door and finding his wife there against his expectations. In a 1977 article, W. M. H. Hummelen posited that the wife could only have moved from one place to the next if there were a space behind the stage where she could move unseen. In his 1992 study, however, he revises this view: "I now think that the dialogue between Lippin and his wife's friend is so extraordinarily long (84 lines out of a total of 199 lines) and also in itself of such small interest that it should be interpreted as an attempt by the friend to distract his interest from his wife's movements. This of course implies that these movements are visible."[43] Both theories about the performance are possible; unfortunately, the text does not allow us to draw any definite conclusions on the matter.

In one instance, however, we do have specific information. The manuscript states very clearly that, at least in the performances for which the epilogues of *Esmoreit, Lippin,* and *Blow-in-the-Box* were written, the spectators were seated and they all had to go down stairs in order to leave.[44] Most critics therefore conclude that the performances had to be indoors, presumably because in outdoor performances there is always room for some spectators to stand around the stage.[45]

A recurrent feature in the *abel* plays is the formula "*Waer sidi?*"

('Where are you?'), employed when a speaker addresses a character who has not yet been present or active on the stage. In his 1977 study of performance practice, Hummelen identifies this formula as evidence that the staging permitted actors to enter and exit.[46] In a detailed study of the *abel* plays and several other fifteenth and sixteenth-century plays, K. Iwema notes that the formula appears in varying circumstances.[47] In the later plays, a character is frequently called up who is already on stage but has not been involved in the action yet. Even in the *abel* plays there is such a case. After Esmoreit has introduced Damiet to his father, he has a short exchange with Platus, who voices his accusations against Robert. Immediately after this, Esmoreit calls upon his father: "Where are you high lord, my father?" (l. 966). Most likely, the king has moved to another side of the stage and Esmoreit now re-establishes a dialogue with him. Even when the "Where are you?" formula is not used, many speeches addressed to newly appearing characters start with other identifying phrases like "O Esmoreit" or "O lovely maiden." These may also be cues to call up actors from backstage or actors who were seated unobtrusively at the rear of the stage. On the other hand, it is also possible that actors doubled up in several roles. One critic notes that *Lancelot* never has more than two characters on stage at a time, and that it could be played by only two actors with quick changes of minor pieces of costume.[48] In that case, the addressing formula would help the audience to identify the character of the moment.

## Criticism

Critical discussions of the *abel* plays and farces as a group (though usually excluding *The Debate of Winter and Summer*) generally concentrate on one topic of interest. Textual problems, deeper symbolic meanings, the relationship between the serious plays and their farces, the social and historical background of the plays, and their dramatic structure are separately treated. All of the *abel* plays as well as the farces have been the subject of textual studies by A. Duinhoven. Duinhoven's knowledge of scribal practice is impressive, but his attempts to reconstruct the "original" text or its source often lead him to propose drastic emendations that do not convince all critics. If we posit that the name *Esmoreit* is a corruption from *is moses* and that *Damiet* derives from *termit*, we may suppose that this play is based on the biblical story of Moses and Pharaoh's daughter, with added elements from Maerlant's rhymed Bible. Such a hypothesis does not necessarily clarify the text of the play as we have it.[49] Hope Traver's 1951 article "Religious Implications in the *abele-Spelen* of the Hulthem Manuscript" was among the first studies of the plays as a group, although she excludes *Winter and Summer*.[50] Traver dismisses the view that the plays were primarily secular and proceeds to connect them with nature myths as well as with Christian mysticism in a scholarly tradition running from Jessie Weston and Robert Graves to R. S. Loomis. As a result, in *Lancelot of Denmark*, Sandrine becomes Summer, exiled to the underworld until the old year (Lancelot) has died and the new year (the Hunter) has claimed her. At the same time, according to Traver, the episode at the fountain recalls "the apocryphal Life of the Virgin which C. B. Lewis sees behind the Old French Weaving Songs and the theme of the Girl at the Fountain."[51] Similarly, she sees the plots of *Esmoreit* and *Gloriant* as transformations of Christian myths—with Esmoreit's foray into the the dungeon to free his mother as a parallel to Christ's Harrowing of Hell. Although Traver was perhaps the first critic to see more than wild and primitive stories in the *abel* plays and her suggestions are intriguing, the plays seem more likely to reflect traditional medieval epics and romances overlaid with occasional Biblical allusions.

Later critics offer interpretations less sweeping than Traver's insistence on the influence of Christian mysticism in the *abel* plays. Some have connected individual details in the plays with elements of Franciscan spirituality, such as the appeal by Esmoreit's mother to the crucified Christ, which sounds like a meditation in its enumeration of specific details:

Mighty God on whom all depends
Undeserving and without guilt
You were nailed onto a tree
God of meekness, *with three nails* (lines 390–93, emphasis mine)

*Ay gheweldich god daer al an staet*
*Ghi waert sonder verdiente ende sonder scout*
*Vaste ghenaghelt ane ene hout*
*Oetmoedech god met naghelen drie.*

Although earlier depictions of the crucifixion usually show Christ attached to the cross with four nails, from the thirteenth century on the use of three nails is more common.[52] The dissemination of this iconographic detail is usually connected with the *Meditationes Vitae Christi* attributed to the so-called Pseudo-Bonaventure.[53]

In her search for deeper symbolic meanings, Traver also overstates the relationship between the *abel* play and its accompanying farce. The closest connection is between *Esmoreit* and *Lippin*, which both show an "unequal marriage" (Pleij uses the term "*ongelijke liefde*") between an older man and younger wife, though the plots are not otherwise related.[54] The connection between the other *abel* plays and their farces is less clear-cut. In all cases, however, the farces present a mood that contrasts with that of the serious plays. Where the latter show an exalted and idealized love between men and women, the farces present a common, often brutal, battle of the sexes, and are especially critical of assertive, sexually active women and the weak men who fail to control them.

In a 1961 critique of Traver's article, N. C. H. Wijngaards points to the fundamental problem in Traver's use of the term "religious implications" in her study.[55] Wijngaards argues that when Traver limits herself to detecting religious implications (echoes, allusions, suggestive elements), her study is quite valuable. When she moves on to argue that the plays are actually transformations of Christian myths, however, she distorts the texts. While praising Traver's attention to the cultural background and context of the plays, Wijngaards also pleads for closer study of another part of that background, namely, Andreas Capellanus' treatise on *fin'amor*. Juxtaposing passages from *Lancelot of Denmark* and *Gloriant* with passages from Andreas' treatise, Wijngaards highlights *Gloriant's* words (after his "conversion" to love):

Now I'm at the mercy of all women
Because for one I languish  (lines 428–29)

*Nu comic te ghenaden allen vrouwen*
*Om ene die mi quelen doet*

Wijngaards claims that these lines resemble a passage from *De amore* (cap. 60): "*pro una omnium debet feminarum servitor existere atque devotus.*"[56] Ironically, Wijngaards slips into the same mistake that he identifies in Traver's work: by the end of his study, *fin'amor* has become the major theme of *Lancelot of Denmark* and *Gloriant*, rather than one element in their cultural background.

There are two major weaknesses in Wijngaards' treatment of *fin'amor* and of Andreas' text as its dogma. In the first place, the meaning and importance of the concept of *fin'amor* and of Andreas' text (known as the *De Amore* in P. G. Walsh's edition and English translation) have been questioned from many perspectives for decades. In *The Meaning of Courtly Love*, a collection of papers presented at a conference held on this topic in Binghamton in 1967, D. W. Robertson calls the concept of courtly love "inherently absurd" and "an impediment to the understanding of medieval texts."[57] Similarly, John F. Benton looks at archival material on love, marriage, and sexual mores and finds it to be incompatible with the so-called "tenets" of courtly love on historical grounds.[58] Indeed, few critics would now maintain that the *De Amore* lays out what was an actual philosophy and practice at the court of Marie de Champagne or any other medieval court.[59] In his introduction to the *De Amore*, Walsh characterizes Andreas Capellanus as a playful commentator on stylized behavior rather than as a law-giver to a historical court. In any case, the situation at a twelfth-century noble court would not be identical to that of a fourteenth-century urban milieu.

The second problem with Wijngaards' reading of the importance of this treatise for the *abel* plays is addressed by N. de Paepe in his 1964 critique of Wijngaards' article.[60] De Paepe points out that the dramatic conflict in *Lancelot of Denmark* does not concern the primacy of nobility of character over nobility of birth, but the fact that Lancelot wants to make Sandrine his mistress rather than his wife.[61] Andreas Capellanus, on the other hand, does not include marriage in his discussion because, in his view, love and marriage are fundamentally incompatible.

Until recently, the farces have received little attention and they are often omitted from editions of the individual *abel* plays, but Pleij's studies on urban culture have focused more attention on the farces as a part of the civilizing process taking place in the towns.[62] Pleij points to lines from the *"Beginsel van allen spelen"* ('A Beginning for all plays') preserved elsewhere in the Van Hulthem manuscript to illustrate one underlying function of the farces:

> You'll find many instructive examples,
> Even though they play the fool;
> They show good sense.
> Now listen and try to understand.

> *Men vint exempel herde vele,*
> *Al eest datse sotte spelen,*
> *Daer subtijlheit leghet ane.*
> *Nu hoert ende pijnt u te verstane.*[63]

In a similar vein, Robert E. Lerner has connected the farces with the *exempla* in the sermons of the friars, and Pleij has even found an *exemplum* containing the story of the farce *Blow-in-the-Box.*[64] Both Lerner and Pleij suggest that the farces are variations on sermons themselves or dramatizations of biblical texts, but other critics, such as the editors of *Truwanten*, see them as entertainment first of all, with instruction as a secondary function.[65]

Many critics attempt to divide the plays into acts or scenes, either on the basis of movements from one location to another or according to divisions suggested by the action. Stuiveling does so as part of a structural analysis of the plays, while others do it silently in editions of individual plays.[66] Although this practice might be useful for organizing a performance, it does not seem necessary for a reading text, which is what all scholarly editions as well as this translation necessarily are.

## The Individual Plays and Farces

## Esmoreit

Esmoreit, infant son of the king of Sicily, is stolen by his cousin Robert, who, disappointed in his expectation to succeed his uncle on the throne, sells the infant to Platus, an astrologer and counselor to the king of Damascus. Platus has been sent to find the child because the stars have shown him that the young prince is destined to kill the king of Damascus and marry his daughter. After the sale, the child's mother, the queen of Sicily, is accused of infanticide and thrown into a dungeon. Meanwhile in Damascus, Esmoreit is treated as a foundling by the king and is entrusted to the care of the princess Damiet. Eighteen years later, Esmoreit hears from Damiet that he is not her brother (as he thought) and he goes off to find his origins. Back in Sicily, the queen recognizes the cloth in which he was originally swaddled (now wrapped around his head). After Esmoreit reveals himself to his father, his mother is freed from prison. Damiet, in love with Esmoreit and impatient for his return, follows him to Sicily in the company of Platus, and they appear just in time to reveal Robert's treachery. The young couple is converted to Christianity and married; the villain is hanged. The threat of Esmoreit killing Damiet's father has been forgotten from the moment when he was first kidnapped.

The theme of the accused queen in general and the play of *Esmoreit* in particular have been discussed in depth by Margaret Schlauch.[67] Her careful study shows that *Esmoreit* is an example of the folk-motif of accused queen stories, which surface both as folk-tales and romances. L. Peeters has pointed to the remarkable correspondences between the plot of *Esmoreit* and the dynastic conflicts between Frederick III of Aragon and Sicily (and his wife Eleonora, daughter of Charles II of Hungary) and his brother Robert of Anjou, which occurred between 1309 and 1321.[68] Schlauch shows, however, that the daughter of the king of Hungary is a recurrent figure in many of the persecuted queen stories, as is the setting in Sicily.[69] In any case, Peeters does not see the historical conflict as the source of *Esmoreit*, but as an inspiration for the recasting of an existing plot.[70]

While accepting Peeters' findings, Duinhoven posits that *Esmoreit* actually derives from the apocryphal story of Moses and Pharaoh's daughter Termit, combined with additional elements from Maerlant's rhymed Bible.[71] Critics have debated the relative importance of the biblical and the historical elements of the plot without coming to a resolution.[72] The Sicilian part of the plot is treated in more detail than that in Damascus, as can be seen when the predicted threat posed by Esmoreit to the king of Damascus is simply forgotten. It is true that Platus has included a reservation in his prediction, saying that the calamitous events will take place "unless a greater providence steps in" (line 83), and the conversions of Esmoreit and Damiet are, of course, signs of a "greater providence," but it is also clear that the action in Sicily is seen to be the important one, Damascus serving as an exotic and more ominous counterpart.

## Lippen
### (*Lippijn*)

Lippin is instructed by his wife to do household chores while she attends mass and goes shopping. In fact, she meets her lover and Lippin observes them by chance, or perhaps because he has followed her (it is not clear which). He complains to his wife's friend ("The Gossip," '*De comere*'), but she manages to convince him that he has seen a mirage and that his wife is actually at home. The text does not explain how the wife manages to get home unseen by Lippin or how the gossip knows that she is already there. When the wife finds out that he has accused her, she scolds him for being a dirty old man and beats him up.

As in *Esmoreit*, the situation of the "unequal lovers" leads to further trouble, though here in a coarser way. Not only is the wife much younger than the husband, but she also bosses him around rather than being led by him as a proper wife should be. Peter Beidler points to similarities between the plot of *Lippin* and that of Chaucer's *Merchant's Tale* and suggests that Chaucer may have been familiar with the Dutch play through his travels.[73]

## Gloriant

Gloriant, Duke of Brunswick, is admonished by his Uncle Gerald and his counselor Geoffrey about the duty of a ruler to marry and produce an heir, but he rejects this advice, saying that no woman is worthy of his attention. Although the elders' arguments are the same as those addressed to Walter in Chaucer's *Clerk's Tale*, the duke's utter rejection of love and women dominates the vivid discussion filled with traditional examples, while the counselors warn the duke against maligning women and provoking Lady Venus' anger.

Far away in pagan Abelant, the maiden Florentine values herself equally highly, but she is aware that one man may be her match, so she sends her messenger Roger to Duke Gloriant with a portrait of herself. Roger fulfills his task and Gloriant is immediately converted to love, much to the astonishment of his uncle. But when Gerald hears that the object of his nephew's love is the daughter of the mighty Red Lion of Abelant, he is horrified. The Red Lion hates the Brunswick family, because relatives have killed the Red Lion's father, uncle, and two of his children. Gloriant cannot be dissuaded, however, and sets off for Abelant. After a violent clash with Florentine's relatives, the couple escapes with the help of Roger, who joins Florentine in converting to Christianity. On their return to Brunswick, they are warmly welcomed by Gerald.

Christian sentiment is especially strong in this play. In his traveling monologue, Gloriant himself attributes his "conversion" to the same love that impelled Christ to his incarnation and redemptive death, and Florentine lectures her father on the crucifixion.[74] When they meet, Gloriant addresses Florentine as *"Spieghel boven alle wiven"*(657), literally "mirror above all women," or "paragon of women," an expression often used to address or describe the Virgin.[75]

In view of the uncertainty about the precise meaning of *abel* ("serious," "handsome," or "artful"), it is remarkable that Florentine is princess of *Abelant* and is said to "bear the palm of noble graces" ('*Si draghet van abelheiden een rijs*,' line 300). Since Gloriant has fallen in love with Florentine just from seeing her portrait, it is not surprising that he attributes noble qualities to her (whatever the exact meaning of *abelheiden* may be). But it is incongruous to see the name *abelant* ("*abel* land") applied to a pagan land with decidedly barbarous customs. Although the possible meanings of *abel* have been discussed extensively, *abelheiden* and *abelant* have not. I suspect that the name may be connected with the (unwarranted) trust and the lack of precaution with which Gloriant sets out for the country and its princess. His misgivings are not voiced until he has arrived there, and even then he and Florentine go to rest in the garden outside the walls without expecting much trouble. But whether the country's name is the result of his trust or its cause is not clear.

A smaller crux in the play is the description of Florentine's portrait which is said to be *gheprent* (line 290), a term which would later come to mean "printed." Since it is unlikely (especially in a fourteenth-century play) that Florentine had a woodcut portrait made (as Hoffmann von Fallersleben states),[76] Leendertz suggests instead that it may have been carved in ivory, like a medallion.[77] Later on, when Florentine sees Gloriant arriving in Abelant, she notes that he has "brought a token before him / By which I recognize him" ('*Hi heeft een teken vore hem bracht / Daer ane dat ickene kinne*,' lines 620–21). This might refer to that medallion which is now worn by Gloriant.

## Blow-in-the-Box
### (*De Buskenblaser*)

A farmer returning from the market, where he sold his cow, is fooled by a peddler into buying a miracle cure to restore his youth. In return for the price of the cow, he is given a box to blow in. When he arrives home he finds that his face is covered with soot. He counters his wife's ridicule by reminding her that she has often reproached him for being old and ugly and that she has dallied with a visiting lay brother.

The same plot also appears in the *Tabula Exemplorum*, a compilation of exempla for the use of preachers.[78] Whether or not this means that the play should be seen strictly as a piece of religious instruction is, of course, open to discussion. The most recent editors have shown that the play is made up of traditional elements, especially in the two opening speeches.[79] The two speakers deliver traditional monologues of the type known as the "*Homme à tout faire*," the boasting young man who wishes to be hired as a servant, as identified by J. C. Aubailly in his study of dramatic genres in the late Middle Ages.[80] The farmer is vulnerable to exploitation because, as an older man with a young wife, he is part of an "unequal marriage." The peddler, with his claim to be able to repair earthenware dishes, is the figure of a quack boasting of outrageous cures. Like *Lippin*, this play seems to end with a fight between the husband and wife.

## Lancelot of Denmark
### (*Lanseloet van Denemerken*)

Prince Lancelot of Denmark declares his love to his mother's lady-in-waiting, Sandrine, and urges her to yield to him. Sandrine, however, tells him first that he is too mighty to marry her, and second that she will not be his mistress. Lancelot's mother, impatient with her weak son, arranges to bring Sandrine into his room, where he rapes her and then turns rudely away as his mother had instructed him to do. When Sandrine emerges, she complains bitterly about his behavior, leaves the court, and wanders into the forest. While she is resting at a spring, she is found by a hunting knight, who, after a long conversation, asks her to marry him.[81] She assents, but not without communicating to him the loss of her virginity in a short fable.

Meanwhile, Lancelot has come to regret his actions. He sends his chamberlain Reynold to search for Sandrine and to tell her that Lancelot now wants to marry her. When the chamberlain finds her, Sandrine declines the offer, repeating to Reynold the fable about the loss of her virginity as a "token" to prove to Lancelot that Reynold actually spoke to her. Reynold returns to court, conveys the message, and Lancelot dies of sorrow and regret.

There was a great deal of familiarity with Arthurian romance in the

Low Countries, as is shown by the fact that "there must have been at least three different Flemish translations of the *Lancelot en prose*."[82] One must assume, then, that the name Lancelot would surely have evoked that well-known paragon of chivalry, thus drawing special attention to the unworthiness of his namesake in the play. It has been suggested that Lancelot's pronouncements on the power of love and its transcendence of differences in social rank are directly influenced by the work of Andreas Capellanus.[83] By the late fourteenth century, however, a straightforward presentation of courtly ideals was no longer likely, but the depiction of the class conflict in the play would reflect the growing self-consciousness of the urban bourgeoisie of that time.

As Van Dijk notes, there is also a contrast between Lancelot's courtly words (though there are some lapses in his courtliness) and his decidedly uncourtly behavior.[84] Although several critics debate whether Lancelot's action constitutes rape or seduction, the text seems to leave no doubt about the issue.[85] Jeannette Koekman has noted how unusual Sandrine is as a character in medieval (or even modern) literature: a rape victim who is not silenced and who takes her fate into her own hands.[86] Several critics have pointed to the play's resemblance to the Biblical story of Amnon and Tamar (2 Samuel 13), with the difference that Amnon is advised by a friend rather than by his mother. The effect of the rape on Amnon's feelings is exactly what Lancelot's mother had hoped for in Lancelot: "Then Amnon hated her exceedingly; so that the hatred wherewith he hated her was greater than the love wherewith he had loved her" (2 Samuel 13:15). In his study of the treatment of time and distance in the *abel* plays, Van Es argues that there is no travel in this play except by characters of secondary importance—everyone except Lancelot. I would argue, however, that the character of Sandrine is of equal importance to Lancelot; the printed edition gives the title of the play as a "very entertaining and amorous story of the noble Lancelot and the lovely Sandrine" ('*Een seer ghenoechlike ende amoreuze historie vanden eedelen Lantsloet ende die scone Sandrijn*'). Sandrine may travel far in the play, as Reynold implies when he tells Lancelot that Sandrine is now living "in a town that is called Rawast. . . It's a town in Africa" ('*In ene stat die heet rawast. . . Ende es in afrijka gheleghen,*' lines 847 and 849). It has been suggested that this is Rabat in present-day Morocco.[87] On the other hand, it is also possible that Reynold simply made up the name of a distant city in order to deter Lancelot from going to look for Sandrine.

Wherever she may be thought to end up, however, there can be no doubt that Sandrine makes a real journey when she leaves the court and moves into the forest. In medieval romances and love poetry, court and forest are often contrasted as the locus of civilized life versus the wilderness. There is a deep irony in Sandrine's move away from the court, the locus of rape, to possible shelter in the forest, the wilderness. The dangers of the forest are made clear in the initially predatory approaches of the unnamed hunting knight. As his conversation becomes more civilized, eventually leading to his proposal of marriage, the knight and Sandrine move to a park (a "*warande*," the word for a private hunting domain) where she accepts his proposal and tells her fable (line 484). The end of the play presents an ambiguous justice: Reynold reports (falsely) that Sandrine has died, and Lancelot dies of remorse. In his dying monologue he blames his mother's counsel as much as his own actions and words. In the epilogue, Reynold advises lovers to speak courteously to their beloved, unlike the way Lancelot treated Sandrine.

## The Witch
## (Die Hexe)

Although the manuscript itself does not give titles to the farces, this play was named "*Die Hexe*" by Hoffman von Fallersleben in his 1838 edition. The word *Hexe* ('witch') did not appear in Dutch until the sixteenth century, but the name has stuck with the play. This farce is the only one that does not pit a deceitful wife against a stupid husband. It opens with two women complaining about their miserable lives: the wool is hard to spin; the cow has run dry; the devil seems to have a hand in all of this. In answer to Machtelt's complaints, Luutgaert remembers seeing an old hag on a crossroads, a certain Juliane, who has recently moved into the area after having been banished from Ghent for theft. Immediately becoming suspicious, the two women pay a visit to Juliane, persuade themselves that she is an agent of the devil, and then proceed to pummel her.

With hardly any plot to speak of in its 110 lines, the play raises many questions but presents only partial answers. In the most recent edition of the farce in the collection *Klein kapitaal uit het handschrift-Van Hulthem*, J. Vromans summarizes the results of several studies. The play contains a number of apparent commonplaces of the time: that the failure of a cow to produce milk was the work of the devil, that witches and ghosts had a need for butter to prepare their dishes, that witches had a preference for dwelling at a crossroads, and that the hand of a thief had magic properties.[88] Vromans also notes that the play is still open to different interpretations, especially if one manages to ignore the title imposed by Hoffmann von Fallersleben. Is the play an indictment of rural superstition? Is Juliane a fraud or a visionary? Orlanda S. H. Lie shows convincingly that for a medieval audience the two women's accusations would clearly point to black magic. On the other hand, Juliane's answers show a remarkable knowledge of magic tricks.[89] Lie sees the farce as ridicule of the belief in black magic and of the danger of easy accusations of witchcraft, but this view does not explain why Juliane encourages the other women with her knowing comments. While Traver had seen *The Witch* as an echo of Lancelot's witch-like mother, this view now seems unlikely. Not only is Lancelot's mother merely evil rather than a witch, but the farce leaves us uncertain as to which of the three women is most to be condemned.

## The Debate of Winter and Summer
### (Vanden Winter ende Vanden Somer)

The fourth of the *abel* plays has, until recently, attracted less interest and admiration than the other three. A debate poem with allegorical characters, it seems far removed from modern aesthetic values. It is also quite different from the other *abel* plays and Van Dijk suggests that it may have been even more different before it was grouped with the other texts, where any similarities that do exist were added by the "adaptor-stage director."[90] This is Van Dijk's term for the unknown writer who was responsible for adding the prologues and epilogues that often tell the audience the moral of the play. That these lines were added after the plays were written is shown at the end of *Blow-in-the-Box*, for instance, where they follow *after* the line count for the play itself. The comments at the end of the *abel* play announcing the farce were probably connected with a specific performance of the play followed by its farce, yet these prologues and epilogues were added before they were included in the Van Hulthem manuscript.

In *The Debate of Winter and Summer*, Summer and Winter both pride themselves on the qualities of their seasons and each claims superiority over the other. Summer makes the birds sing and the flowers bloom and instills joy in the people who play the game of love. Winter has the power to silence the birds, imprison the fish under the ice, and bring chattering teeth and chapped hands. Summer produces the riches of the earth; Winter consumes them.

The vassals of Winter and Summer enter into the argument: Lazybones (*Loiaert*) and Handsome (*Moiaert*) on behalf of Summer, and Blabber (*Clappaert*) and Braggart (*Bollaert*) on behalf of Winter, each arguing that love is more "*noyael*," more courteous and courtly, in their favorite season. The conflict reaches a climax when Winter challenges Summer to a duel for the honor of Lady Venus, and Summer accepts his challenge. Here a fifth character known as the Tramp (*Die cockijn*) steps in. The Tramp hates Winter and offers to be a security for Summer "with all his goods"—a comic touch, since the Tramp has described himself as having been brought to ruin by Winter and he appears to be barely covered in rags. His offer is scornfully rejected, and Blabber and Handsome are chosen to be the guarantors for their respective lords.

All the characters leave the stage except Handsome, who is the one who is most concerned with the course of events. He sees that there is really no possibility of a good outcome to this conflict and decides to go to Lady Venus and beg her for help, since the conflict concerns her. Lady Venus promises to lend her assistance. As Van Dijk has pointed out, this means that a different outcome to the conflict has now become possible, but only Handsome and the audience are aware of it, thereby creating dramatic irony.[91]

The next morning, as the two combatants position themselves for the fight, Lady Venus appears and commands them to stop. She explains that Winter and Summer are brothers made by God, as is everything in this world, including the stars and the planets that govern the alternation of each of the seasons according to nature. Lady Venus stops further argument and invites everyone to eat, drink, and be joyful. Only the Tramp is left to complain bitterly that Winter will still be around, and he decides to depart for the coal mines of Maastricht to take refuge in the vagrants' camp.

Critics have pointed to the long tradition of *conflictus* poetry, but Van Dijk was the first to distinguish clearly between the scholarly Latin tradition, exemplified by the *Conflictus Veris et Hiemis* dating from the eighth century, and the folk tradition, which was described by Dirc van Delft, chaplain at the court of The Hague from 1399 to 1404.[92] In his discussion of the Redemption, bridging the Winter Piece and the Summer Piece of the *Tafel van Kersten Ghelove* ('Table of the Christian Faith'), Dirc comes to the fourth Sunday of Lent, also called *Laetare* ('rejoice') Sunday after the first word of the Introit of the Mass on that day. Dirc notes that both the approach of Easter and that of the Spring season are reasons for joy: "For this reason, the clerks in these regions on this Sunday commonly act out Winters and Summers. And Winter is made rough and harshly fearful and Summer green and newly cheerful, forceful in speaking and battling. But Winter, with his freezing, must yield and lose, for Summer begins to appear, whom all sensible people prefer."[93] These ceremonies took place all over Europe and, although no written text dating before 1576 is known to survive, data gathered by W. Liungman indicate that they were seasonal and therefore, if set in Spring, would be expected to end with the defeat of Winter.[94] The prologue of our play also specifies this setting:

> Summer is on his way
> So know that he is coming

> *Die somer hi es int gheride*
> *Ende weet dat hi comen sal* (lines 16–17)

The scholarly tradition knew different forms of the debate between the seasons. H. Walther's study of medieval Latin debate poems, for example, prints one version in which Lady Theology imposes an end to the dispute.[95]

Although it is useful to trace the scholarly tradition, which goes back to Virgil's Third Eclogue, and note the common themes of the genre, it is also clear that the scholarly and the popular strains were closely connected from the beginning. This is not surprising, since the popular ceremonies were also performed by clerks. Many arguments recur in several texts, such as who is Lord (*Heer*) and who is Vassal (*Knecht*) and the fact that Summer produces the riches that Winter consumes. The *abel* play puts unusual stress on the role of Love and its courtliness, but in many other poems love plays a part as well. In the *Conflictus Veris et Hiemis*, the arbiter Palemon welcomes the cuckoo with the greeting "tu iam dulcis amor" ('thou art Love himself' in Waddell's translation). This cuckoo (*cuculus*) is the harbinger of Spring, almost a personification of Spring in many of the Latin poems, welcomed by Summer because he brings light and flowers, reviled by Winter because he breaks the peace and quiet of his sleep by the fire. It has been suggested that the odd figure of the *cockijn*, a tramp among the noble courtiers, is related to the traditional *cuculus*.[96]

In his study of debate poetry, Thomas L. Reed distinguishes between horizontal debates between equal partners and vertical ones between an authority figure and a naive interlocutor, and discusses the various ways in which the poems achieve a final resolution.[97] Frequently, a resolution is imposed from above by an authority figure (like Venus in our play), who reveals a form of Divine Reason that is not always clearly visible to man. Reed notes the occurrence of another element as well: "the occasional reflex to 'subvert' the serious, dialectical quest for a single truth that seems a given of disputation. This subversion at times takes the form of irreverent and disruptive humor . . . and quite frequently involves an outright refusal to reach a conclusion in the terms of the original quest."[98] Perhaps the disreputable *cockijn* fulfills this function when, in the last words of the play and following Venus' solemn pronouncement, he expresses his displeasure with the peaceful end to the conflict, preferring life in the vagrants' camp to life at the court of Venus.

## Ruben

A young man announces to his parents-in-law that their daughter has just been delivered of a full-term baby and expresses some doubt about his role in the event, which took place after only three months of marriage. The mother-in-law manages to convince him that he has miscalculated the length of the marriage, and the young man goes home to apologize to his wife. The father-in-law, who has ostensibly supported his wife in her arguments, attacks her and all women after Ruben's departure, and the play seems to end in another fight between a man and wife.

Strietman has pointed out that the argument of this farce is a direct inversion of Lady Venus' high moral speech about God's ordering of the seasons.[99] This interpretation creates a stronger connection between these two plays than between the other *abel* plays and their farces.

## The Translation

This translation uses Van Kammen's text (*De Abele Spelen*, 1968) as its basis. When questions arose, I compared the text both with other recent editions such as those in *Klein Kapitaal uit het Handschrift-Van-Hulthem* (1992) and with a microfilm of the manuscript provided by the Bibliothèque Royale Albert I in Brussels. A sample of the original Middle Dutch text has been provided in the Appendix for purposes of comparison with the present translation.

As was noted in the discussion of *The Witch*, the manuscript does not give titles to the farces or lists of characters for any of the plays. Traditionally, titles made up by the earliest editors have been used ever since. The lists of personages are derived from the various texts, but their names frequently change during the course of the play. In *Esmoreit*, for instance, the king of Damascus is simply called "the King." The first time the king of Sicily appears he is called "the Christian King" ('*de kersten coninc*'); later he is just called "the king" until Esmoreit returns from Damascus, when he is again called "the Christian king." The queen of Sicily is called "The Lady" ('*de vrouwe*') when she is accused of adultery. When she has been freed by Esmoreit's intercession, she is sometimes called "his mother" ('*sine moeder*'). Damiet is sometimes called "the young lady Damiet" ('*de jonge joncfrouwe Damiet*') and Platus is always called "the Master" ('*de meester*') in the rubrics. For the convenience of the reader, these appellations have been standardized in the translation.

In the farces there seems to be no attempt at consistency in giving names to some characters and not to others. In *Ruben,* for instance, the father-in-law is called Gosen and the mother-in-law is called "the wife" (Ruben's wife does not appear). In *Blow-in-the-Box,* the text refers to "the first man," "the other man," and "his wife." After the wife has appeared, the first man is called "the first man her man/husband" (the Dutch word *man* means both "man" and "husband"). The wife calls on "Gert, dear neighbor" ('*Gheert lieve ghebure,*' whom Van Kammen takes to be a female, but later critics to be a male), and the rubrics list this person as "Gert his neighbor." When there are English equivalents to the names (Godevaert—Geoffrey, Robbrecht—Robert, Rogier—Roger), I have adopted them. In other cases I have sometimes adapted the spelling slightly for ease of pronunciation, as in "Lippin" for Middle Dutch "Lippijn." I have also added indications in brackets when the action jumps from one time or place to another, such as: [Damascus, eighteen years later] in *Esmoreit* after line 405.

The texts in the manuscript have virtually no punctuation. This often creates an ambiguity with respect to some clauses that can be taken as referring both to the line preceding them as well as to the following line. This ambiguity proved to be too confusing to maintain in an English reading text, but I have tried to be sparing in my use of periods and commas. In translating, I have stayed very close to the original Dutch texts, but I have not tried to reproduce the rhymes. To make up for the absence of rhyme and provide not only a reading text but also one that can be read aloud in a staged performance, I have regularized the lengths of the lines somewhat.

# Notes

1. "Acheté à la vente des livres de M. Nuewens, notaire à Bruxelles, faite en avril 1811." C. P. Serrure, who was the first to mention the inscription in his "Het Groot Hulthemsch Handschrift," *Vaderlandsch Museum* (1859–60), III, 139–164, comments that the scantiness of the information on the manuscript at the time is not surprising in view of the low esteem of Netherlandic history and literature during the French occupation of the Low Countries (1794–1814). Further information is provided by W. van Anrooij, "Bijdrage tot een Geografische Situering van het Handschrift Van Hulthem," *Spiegel der Letteren*, 28 (1986), 4.

2. The first careful description of the manuscript can be found in P. Leendertz, ed., *Middelnederlandsche Dramatische Poëzie* (Leiden, 1907), pp. i–xi. Additional textual details are given in L. van Kammen, ed., *De Abele Spelen* (Amsterdam, 1968), pp. 7–9 and 23–29. The most recent information is in W. van Anrooij, "Bijdrage tot een Geografische Situering van het Handschrift Van Hulthem," *Spiegel der Letteren*, 28 (1986), 225–33. The comments here are taken from Leendertz unless otherwise indicated.

3. This number actually represents a series of numbers, because the Royal Library generally assigns a signature to each separate work in a collection. The series of numbers suggests that there are 34 separate texts in the manuscript, while the original numbering in the manuscript gives 214 items. The actual number is somewhat larger, as some numbers comprise more than one text. Of the plays which concern us, for instance, *Esmoreit* is number 169, *Lippin* is number 170, *Gloriant* and *Blow-in-the-Box* together are number 205, *Lancelot of Denmark* and *The Witch* are number 206, and *The Debate of Winter and Summer* and *Ruben* are number 211. A full listing of all the texts in the collection is given in H. van Dijk et al., eds., *Klein Kapitaal uit het Handschrift-Van Hulthem* (Hilversum, 1992), pp. 12–20.

4. H. van Dijk et al., eds., *Klein Kapitaal uit het Handschrift-Van Hulthem*, p. 9. On *littera cursiva* and *littera textualis*, see D. Greetham, *Textual Scholarship: An Introduction* (New York and London, 1992), pp. 170–71.

5. H. Pleij, "Volksfeest en toneel in de middeleeuwen," *Revisor*, 4 (1977), 34–41. The art workshops are discussed by L. Campbell, "The Art Market in the Southern Netherlands in the Fifteenth Century," *The Burlington Magazine*, 118:2 (April 1976), 188–98.

6. The word *tconincx* is frequently emended to *sconincx*, 'the king's, but in this case the manuscript has a clear *t*.

7. All editions except Van Kammen's (1968) emend *moerder* ('murderer') to *moeder* ('mother'). As Van Kammen notes, however, the slip of the pen is interesting because Lancelot's mother is, indeed, indirectly responsible for his death (see note, p. 163).

8. There are two other plays (numbers 209 and 210, found between *Lancelot of Denmark* and *The Debate of Winter and Summer*) in the same part of the manuscript. They are not included here because the manuscript is now missing two to four leaves. As a result, the first play, of which 405 lines remain, is missing either 135 or 375 lines, more likely the latter. The second play, which according to the line count should have 196 lines, starts at line 104. The first, generally called *Drie Daghe Here* ("Lord for Three Days") has the rubric *"Ene sotte boerde ende ene goede sotternie"* ('A funny joke and a good farce'). Thematically, it is similar to the other farces, but it must have been considerably longer and more like the *abel* plays in terms of length and plot development. The second play, called *Truwanten* ("Beggars" or "Vagrants"), must have been similar in length to the farces.

9. The manuscript reads *"Een abel spel ende een edel dinc"* ('an *abel* play and noble tale') in the case of *Gloriant*.

10. Grimm, *Deutsches Wörterbuch*, vol. 10, especially article 3.

11. Van Anrooij and Van Buuren, "'s Levens Felheid in een Band: Het Handschrift-Van Hulthem," in *Op Belofte van Profijt*, ed. H. Pleij (Amsterdam, 1991), pp. 190–92; Van Anrooij, "Bijdrage tot een Geografische Situering van het Handschrift Van Hulthem," *Spiegel der Letteren*, 28 (1986), and "29 September 1399," in *Nederlandse Literatuur, een Geschiedenis*, ed. M. A. Schenkeveld-van der Dussen et al. (1993), pp. 86–91.

12. P. Leendertz, ed., p. iii.

13. *Hier beghint een seer ghenoechlike ende amoroeze historie vanden eedelen Lantsloet ende die scone Sandrijn* ('Here begins a very pleasant and amorous story of the noble Lancelot and the lovely Sandrine') was published by Govert van Ghemen between 1486 and 1492. A facsimile of this book, belonging to the Bibliothek der Hansestadt in Lübeck (Germany), was published by M. Nijhoff in 1902.

14. An extensive description of these texts as well as a bibliography can be found in R. Roemans and H. van Assche, eds., *Een Abel Spel van Lanseloet van Denemerken*, 2nd ed. (Amsterdam, 1963).

15. Wim N. M. Hüsken and Frans A. M. Schaars, eds., *Sandrijn en Lanslot: Diplomatische uitgave van twee toneelrollen uit het voormalig archief van de Rederijkerskamer De Fiolieren te's-Gravenpolder* (Nijmegen-Grave, 1985), pp. 3–10.

16. *Messager des Sciences et des Arts de la Belgique*, (Gand [Ghent], 1835), III, 6–40.

17. H. Hoffmann von Fallersleben, ed., *Horae Belgicae*, (Breslau, 1838), Vol. 6; H. E. Moltzer, ed., *De Middelnederlandsche Dramatische Poëzie* (Groningen, 1868–75); P. Leendertz, ed., *Middelnederlandsche Dramatische Poëzie* (Leiden, 1899–1907); L. van Kammen, ed., *De Abele Spelen* (Amsterdam, 1968).

18. *An Ingenious Play of Esmoreit, the King's Son of Sicily*, trans. H. M. Ayres, intro. by A. Barnouw (The Hague, 1924); *A Beautiful Play of Lancelot of Denmark, How He Fell in Love with a Lady Who Waited upon His Mother*, trans. P. Geyl (The Hague, 1924); "A Fine Play of Lancelot, How He Came to Woo a Damsel Who Was in His Mother's Service," trans. E. Colledge, in *Reynard the Fox and Other Mediaeval Netherlands Secular Literature* (London, 1967); *An Excellent Play of Esmoreit, Prince of Sicily*, trans. J. Oakshott and E. Strietman, in *Dutch Crossings: A Journal of Low Countries Studies* 30 (1986), 3–39; "Three *Sotterniën*, Farcical Afterpieces from the Hulthem Manuscript," trans. Therese Decker and Martin Walsh, in *Dutch Crossings: A Journal of Low Countries Studies*, 48 (Autumn 1992), 73–96. Decker and Walsh give different titles than those used here: *Lippijn, The Boxblower*, and *Rubben*. Most recently: *Netherlandic Secular Plays from the Middle Ages; the "Abele Spelen" and Farces of the Hulthem Manuscript*, Trans. Theresia de Vroom (Ottawa, 1997).

19. *Yearbook of Comparative and General Literature*, 35 (1986), 56–104.

20. Eckehard Simon is currently editing a large collection of performance records pertaining to secular drama in German-speaking regions of Europe.

21. Eckehard Simon, ed. *The Theater of Medieval Europe: New Research in Early Drama* (Cambridge, 1991). I owe a great debt to Elsa Strietman's article on "The Low Countries" (pp. 225–52). Her bibliography should be the first resource for anyone studying the subject.

22. Authoritative, though sometimes opposing, views are collected in F. X. Newman, ed., *The Meaning of Courtly Love* (Albany, 1968). Roger Boase gives a

critical survey of scholarship on the subject in *The Origin and Meaning of Courtly Love* (Manchester, 1977). A more recent array of views is presented in Robert R. Edwards and Stephen Spector, eds., *The Olde Daunce: Love, Friendship, Sex and Marriage in the Medieval World* (Albany, 1991). See also below, CRITICISM, for the work of N. C. H. Wijngaards and N. de Paepe.

23. On the opposition between *vilein* and *courtois*, see K. Gravdal, *Vilain et Courtois* (Lincoln, Neb., 1991), pp. 12–19. Although Gravdal writes about an earlier period, her tracing of the two terms is illuminating. Like *vilain*, the word *dorper* denotes first a person from the countryside, a worker of the soil, a peasant. Soon, the words come to denote lack of manners and lack of morality. The opposite to *dorper* (and the adverb *dorperlike* and noun *dorpernie*) is *hovesch*, that is: 'related to the *hof*, the court,' or *noyael*. These words occur frequently in the *abel* plays: *hovesch* or *hoveschelike*, for instance, occurs nine times in the 952 lines of *Lancelot of Denmark*; *dorpernie* and *dorperheit* occur eight times.

24. Excerpts from the records of the court at The Hague have been published by W. J. A. Jonckbloet, *Geschiedenis van den Middelnederlandsche Dichtkunst* (Amsterdam, 1851–55), III, 593–652. For other locations, see H. van Dijk in *Nederlandse Literatuur: Een Geschiedenis*, ed. M. A. Schenkeveld-van der Dussen et al. (Groningen, 1993), pp. 62–67, and references there.

25. *Het Literaire Leven in de Middeleeuwen* (Leiden, 1988), pp. 74–77.

26. Marcel Vanhamme, *Bruxelles, de Bourg Rural à Cité Mondiale* (Anvers/Bruxelles, 1968), p. 76. This is a considerably larger population than that of either Brueges or Ghent, each of which ranged from 10,000 to 20,000 inhabitants. London is estimated to have had about 35,000 inhabitants in 1390; see M. Gilbert, *British History Atlas* (London, 1968), p. 27.

27. On the "unequal marriage," see W. A. Coupe, "Ungleiche Liebe: A Sixteenth Century Topos," *Modern Language Review*, 62 (1967), 661–71, and Alison Stewart, *Unequal Lovers: A Study of Unequal Couples in Northern Art* (New York, 1978).

28. Pleij, *Het Literaire Leven*, p. 75.

29. *Chaucer's Constance and Accused Queens* (1927; rpt. New York, 1969).

30. In Wolfram von Eschenbach's *Willehalm*, Guibour appears as Gyburc and is also converted.

31. J. A. Worp, *Geschiedenis van het Wereldlijk Tooneel in Nederland, gedurende de Middeleeuwen* (Rotterdam, 1970), pp. 75–80.

32. See Michel Olsen, "Les Miracles de Nostre Dame par Personnages," in *Popular Drama in Northern Europe in the Later Middle Ages*, ed. F. G. Andersen et al. (Odense, 1988), pp. 41–63.

33. See their edition of *Lanseloet van Denemerken* (1966), pp. xix–xxiii.

34. David F. Johnson, ed. and trans., *Penninc and Pieter Vostaert: Roman van Walewein* (New York, 1992), pp. xv–xxi.

35. Van Dijk discusses several of the breaks in the straddling rhyme in detail in "The Structure of the Sotternieën in the Hulthem Manuscript," in *The Theater in the Middle Ages*, ed. H. Braet et al. (Leuven, 1985), pp. 238–50. One example is from *Blow-in-the-Box*, when the man asks for a mirror to look at his face. The wife agrees—in a single line—and one may well imagine a pause in the action during which the man reacts to seeing his face covered with soot before speaking again (Van Dijk, p. 242).

36. Garmt Stuiveling, "De Structuur van de Abele Spelen," in *Vakwerk: Twaalf Studies in Literatuur* (Zwolle, 1967), pp. 7–43.

37. Stuiveling, pp. 41 and 284. On changing aesthetic perceptions, see Olsen's comments in relation to the *Miracles de Nostre Dame par personnages* (1988), pp. 42–43.

38. Although Van Es begins his article by speculating briefly about staging practices, his argument is mainly about the alternation of different ideological spheres and not about staging areas.

39. Van Es, pp. 172–73.

40. Van Es, pp. 183–85.

41. See Erik Kooper, ed., *Medieval Dutch Literature in its European Context* (Cambridge, 1994), pp. 290–91.

42. See Hüsken and Schaars, eds., *Sandrijn en Lanslot* (Nijmegen-Grave, 1985), p. 4 and note.

43. "Tekst en Toneelinrichting in de Abele Spelen," *De Nieuwe Taalgids*, 70 (1977), 229–42, and "Performers and Performance in the Earliest Serious Secular Plays in the Netherlands," *Comparative Drama*, 26 (1992), 19–33.

44.    Everyone remain seated in peace
       No one should go home.
       A farce we will play for you;
       It'll be short, I tell you.
       Let whoever is hungry go and eat
       And all go down those stairs.
       If you liked it, come back tomorrow.

       Elc blive sittene in sinen vrede
       Niemen en wille thuus weert gaen
       Ene sotheid sal men u spelen gaen
       Die cort sal sijn doe ic u weten
       Wie hongher heeft hi mach gaen eten
       Ende gaet alle dien graet neder
       Ghenoeghet u soe comt alle mergen weder (*Esmoreit*, lines 1012–18)
       Get up, you may leave now.
       Staet op ghi moghet wel gaen voert (*Lippin*, line 197)

       Good people, this play is done;
       You can all go home now.
       Let all go down the stairs.
       If you liked it, come back tomorrow.

       Ghi goede liede dit spel is ghedaen
       Ghi mochte wel alle thuus weert gaen
       Ende lopen alle den graet neder
       Ghenoeghet u comt alle weder (*Blow-in-the-Box*, lines 205–8)

45. See also Van Dijk, "De Graaf van Blois Bezoekt een Zoldertheater in Dordrecht," in *Nederlandse Literatuur, een Geschiedenis*, ed. M. A. Van Schenkeveld-van Dussen et al. (1993), pp. 62–67. Van Dijk was the first to suggest that the performance might also have been on a raised stage outdoors.

46. "Tekst en Toneelinrichting in de Abele Spelen," p. 233. Hummelen also summarizes the older opinions of Leendertz and other critics.

47. K. Iwema, *"Waer sidi*—over een Middelnederlandse Toneelconventie,"
*Nieuwe Taalgids*, 77 (1984), 48–61. Among the plays studied by Iwema are the
two "Joys of Mary" plays, *Elckerlijc* ('Everyman'), and several later Rhetoricians'
plays.

48. N. H. C. Wijngaards, "Structuurvergelijking bij de Abele Spelen," *Levende
Talen*, 43 (1962), 322–27.

49. A. M. Duinhoven, "De Bron van *Esmoreit*," *De Nieuwe Taalgids*, 72 (1979),
124–44.

50. *The Germanic Review*, 26 (1951), 34–49.

51. Traver, pp. 37–38. The reference is to C. B. Lewis' article, "The Origin of
the Weaving Songs and the Theme of the Girl at the Fountain," *PMLA*, 37
(1922), 141. Lewis' reading of the so-called "Weaving Songs" has been largely
rejected by more recent critics.

52. L. Réau, *Iconographie de l'art chrétien* (Paris, 1955–59), II, 480–81.

53. Roza van Hoogenbeemt, "De Voorstelling van de Gekruisigde van de XIIe
tot de XVIIe Eeuw," *Ons Geestelijk Erf*, 22 (1948), 201–36.

54. On "unequal marriage," see note 25 above.

55. N. C. H. Wijngaards, "Andreas Capellanus' *De Arte Honeste Amandi* en de
Abele Spelen," *Spiegel der Letteren*, 5 (1961), 218–28.

56. Wijngaards, pp. 226–27.

57. D. W. Robertson, Jr., "The Concept of Courtly Love as an Impediment to
the Understanding of Medieval Texts," in *The Meaning of Courtly Love*, ed. F. X.
Newman (Albany, 1968), pp. 1–18; for Newman's synopsis, see pp. viii–ix.

58. John F. Benton, "Clio and Venus: An Historical View of Medieval Love,"
in *The Meaning of Courtly Love*, ed. F. X. Newman (Albany, 1968), pp. 19–42.

59. For several different views, see the essays collected in *The Meaning of Courtly
Love*, ed. F. X. Newman (Albany, 1968), and n. 22 above.

60. "Kunnen Onze Beatrijslegende en Abele Spelen Geëvalueerd Worden door
Middel van Andreas Capellanus' *De Arte Honeste Amandi?*" *Leuvense Bijdragen*, 53
(1964), 120–47.

61. This had already been pointed out by J. van Mierlo in "Het Dramatisch Conflict in Lanseloet van Denemerken," *Verslagen en Mededelingen van de Koninklijke Vlaamsche Academie voor Taal- en Letterkunde* (1942), pp. 339–57.

62. Pleij, *De Sneeuwpoppen van 1511* (Amsterdam, 1988), pp. 131 ff.; see also note 25 above.

63. Leendertz, ed., pp. 442–43 (lines 49–52), quoted in H. Pleij, "De Sociale Funktie van Humor en Trivialiteit op het Rederijkerstoneel," *Spektator*, 5 (1975–76), 120.

64. R. Lerner, "Vagabonds and Little Women," *Modern Philology*, 65 (1968), 301–306; H. Pleij, "Hoe Interpreteer Je een Middelnederlandse Tekst," *Spektator*, 6 (1976–77), 346–47. The *exemplum* is found in J. Th. Welter's edition of the *Tabula Exemplorum secundum ordinem Alphabeti: Recueil d'Exempla compilé en France à la fin du xiiie siècle* (1927; rpt. Geneva, 1973), p.17, number 50.

65. Werkgroep Brusselse en Utrechtse Neerlandici, *Truwanten*, pp. 102–107.

66. Garmt Stuiveling, "De Structuur van de Abele Spelen," *Vakwerk* (1967); Roemans and Gaspar's edition of *Gloriant* is divided into acts on the basis of themes.

67. *Chaucer's Constance and Accused Queens* (1927; rpt. 1963).

68. L. Peeters, "*Esmoreit sconinx sone van Cecielien*: Siciliaanse Historie als Abel Spel," *Spiegel der Letteren*, 19 (1977), 245–79.

69. Schlauch, pp. 69–73 and 119.

70. Peeters (1977), p. 248.

71. A. M. Duinhoven, "De Bron van *Esmoreit*," *De Nieuwe Taalgids*, 72 (1979), 124–44. Earlier, Duinhoven had studied the textual problems of *Esmoreit* in "Pleidooi voor een reconstructie van *Esmoreit*," *Spiegel der Letteren*, 17 (1979), 241–67.

72. A. L. I. Sivirsky, "De Stamboom van Esmoreit," *Spiegel der Letteren*, 20 (1978), 257–65; L. Peeters, "*Esmoreit* in het Geding," *Spiegel der Letteren*, 20 (1978), 266–72; H. Pleij, "Over de Betekenis van Middelnederlandse Teksten," *Spektator*, 10 (1980–81), 299–339; A. M. Duinhoven, "Van Moses tot Esmoreit," *Spektator*, 10 (1980–81), 566–76.

73. Peter G. Beidler and Therese Decker, "*Lippijn*: A Middle Dutch Source for the *Merchant's Tale*?," *The Chaucer Review*, 23 (1989), 236–50.

74. One may compare this to Gyburc's exposition of her Christian faith to her father Terramer in Wolfram's *Willehalm* (215–218).

75. See *Middelnederlandsch Woordenboek*, s.v. *spieghel*, 3. See also, Ritamary Bradley, "Backgrounds of the Title *Speculum* in Mediaeval Literature," *Speculum*, 29 (1954), 100–115. The expression is also used in *Lancelot of Denmark* (line 904).

76. *Horae Belgicae*, VI, 220–21.

77. *Middelnederlandsche Dramatische Poëzie*, pp. 507–508.

78. H. Pleij, "De Sociale Funktie van Humor en Trivialiteit op het Rederijkerstoneel," *Spektator*, 5 (1975–76), 121. For the text of the exemplum, see *Tabula Exemplorum*, ed. J. Th. Welter, pp. 2, 17, 88, 100.

79. An annotated edition of the farce, with discussion and extensive references, is given by H. van Dijk, F. Kramer and J. Tersteeg in *Klein Kapitaal uit het Handschrift-Van Hulthem* (Hilversum, 1992), pp. 164–79. The introduction gives detailed information about the structure and background of the play, from which my comments are derived.

80. J. C. Aubailly, *Le Monologue, le Dialogue et la Sottie: Essai sur quelques genres dramatiques de la fin du Moyen Age et du début du XVIe siècle* (Paris, 1976).

81. The spring ("fonteine") appears as Sandrine is praying for help to Mary, "fountain or well-spring of purity," and "fountain or well-spring of virtues." If one takes her flight into the forest (i.e., into the wilderness, not into some kind of park) seriously, "fonteine" is better translated as "spring" rather than "fountain," and in fact a woodcut in the 1486 incunable edition shows Sandrine standing at a brook and the hunter-knight on his horse on the other side of the water.

82. Bart Besamusca and Orlanda S. H. Lie, "The Prologue to "Arturs Doet'," in *Medieval Dutch Literature in its European Context*, ed. E. Kooper (Cambridge, 1994), pp. 101–102.

83. Wijngaards, "Andreas Capellanus' *De Arte Honeste Amandi* en de Abele Spelen," *Spiegel der Letteren*, 5 (1961), 218–28; Wijngaards' argument is rejected by De Paepe, "Kunnen onze Beatrijslegende en Abele Spelen Geëvalueerd Worden

door Middel van Andreas Capellanus' *De Arte Honeste Amandi?*," *Leuvense Bijdragen*, 53 (1964), 120–47.

84. "*Lansloet van Denemerken*," in *Popular Drama in Northern Europe in the Later Middle Ages*, ed. Andersen (1986), pp. 110–111.

85. Leendertz goes to great lengths to show that Lancelot is the victim of his mother's manipulations, and even more recently Besamusca argues that Lancelot suffers from *amor hereos*, thus rationalizing an act of plain rape. I thank Dr. Besamusca for showing me a copy of his paper in advance of publication; see "*Amor hereos* in Middle Dutch Literature," in *Literary Aspects of Courtly Culture*, ed. D. Maddox and S. Sturm-Maddox (Woodbridge/Rochester, 1994), pp. 189–96.

86. "De Stilte rond Sanderijn," in *De Canon onder Vuur*, ed. E. Van Alphen and M. Meijer (Amsterdam, 1991), pp. 20–34.

87. C. J. H. Steketee, "Rawast in Afrijka," *De Nieuwe Taalgids*, 50 (1957), 330.

88. Vromans, ed. (1992), pp. 181–83.

89. O. S. H. Lie, "*Die Hexe* in het Perspectief van Middelnederlandse Tover-boeken," *Madoc*, 4 (1990), 212–20.

90. H. van Dijk, "Als on die Astrominen lesen: Over het abel spel *Vanden Winter ende vanden Somer*," in *Tussentijds*, ed. A. M. J. Van Buuren et al. (Utrecht, 1985), p. 60.

91. H. van Dijk, "Als ons die Astrominen lesen," p. 63.

92. H. van Dijk, "Als ons die Astrominen lesen," pp. 56–70. For the *Conflictus Veris et Hiemis*, formerly attributed to Alcuin, see Helen Waddell, *Mediaeval Latin Lyrics* (London, 1966), pp. 82–87.

93. "Ende om aldusdanighe saken pleghen die clercken in veel stichten op desen sonnendach winters ende somers te spelen. Ende die winter is ghemaect ruusch ende ruwe vreselic ende die somer groen ende nyeuwe blidelic, mit spreken ende mit striden huechlic. Mer die winter mit sinen vriesen moet wiken ende verliesen. Want die Somer beghint dan te bliken, die alle gheesten dan verkiesen." See, *Somerstuc*, cap. I, 34–41. Dirc sees this battle entirely in symbolic terms: "Summer and Winter shall battle in Our Lord Jesus' heart on Mount Olive as Sin with God's Mercy. Like Winter and Summer, so shall Life

battle against Death, Damnation against the realm of Salvation, the Passion against Nature." ('Die somer ende die winter sellen in ons heren Jhesus herte opten berch van Oliveten vechten, als die sonde ende ghenade Gods. Ghelijc winter ende somer, soe sellen te gader striden dat leven teghen die doot, die verdoemenisse teghen dat rijc der salicheit, die passie ende die natuer'); *Somerstuc*, cap. I, 61–65.

94. W. Liungman, *Der Kampf zwischen Sommer und Winter* (Helsinki, 1941), numbers 3–6, 94–95, 157, and 160. See also L. Uhland, "Sommer und Winter," *Schriften zur Geschichte der Dichtung und Sage* (Stuttgart, 1866), III, 17–51. There are a few examples of these battles taking place in Fall, and these would end in a victory for Winter. An early example of a related debate from a manuscript dating from 1457 is discussed and translated by Leif Sondergaard and Thomas Pettitt, "The Flyting of Yule and Lent," *Early Drama, Art, and Music Review*, 16 (1993), I–II.

95. H. Walther, *Das Streitgedicht in der lateinischen Literatur des Mittelalters* (Munich, 1920), p. 34.

96. K. van der Waerden, "De figuur van de cockijn in het abel spel *Vanden Winter ende vanden Somer*," *Spektator*, 15 (1985–86), 268–77.

97. *Middle English Debate Poetry and the Aesthetics of Irresolution* (Columbia, Mo., 1990).

98. *Middle English Debate Poetry*, p. 21.

99. "The Low Countries," in *The Theater of Medieval Europe*, ed. Eckehard Simon (Cambridge, 1991), p. 227.

# ESMOREIT

## The Characters

The King of Sicily (The Christian King)
The Queen of Sicily (The Lady)
Esmoreit, their son (The Young Man)
Robert, cousin of Esmoreit
The King of Damascus
Master Platus, his counselor and astrologer
Damiet, daughter of the King of Damascus

# An *Abel* Play of Esmoreit

## the King of Sicily's Son

### and a Farce Following It

### [Prologue]

God who was born of the Virgin—
Because he would not lose
What he had made with his hands—
Died his death therefore,
Mothernaked and loyal to us.                                    5
Now I pray you, ladies and gentlemen,
That you will be quiet and listen.
There once was a king—
In Sicily he reigned—
Pay heed and hear these marvels:                               10
He had a child by his wife,
But a scoundrel lived with him,
His brother's son, named Robert.
By right he would inherit
The kingdom in full                                            15
If the king died without an heir,
But now a male child was born
And Robert felt great anger
And great envy in his heart.
Now you will see shortly                                       20
What will happen to the young man:
The sorrow Robert caused him,
Who sold him to a Saracen
And brought him great misery,
And also to the mother who bore him.                           25

She did not smile even once,
Imprisoned for twenty years,
And never saw sun or moon.
Robert brought all that about.
Now be still and watch our play.                    30

*Robert*
Alas for the misfortune,
The birth that has just taken place
Of Esmoreit my cousin.
I fancied myself the king
If my uncle would die;                              35
But now the greybeard has a child
Born to him by his wife.
O Sicily, pleasure garden,
Noble forest, noble realm,
I will remain forever                               40
Bereft of you, noble forest,
A bastard, and with heavy heart,
O, it will be the death of me!
But by God, who is my creator,
For this I'll work day and night:                   45
How I will destroy that child.
I will smother it or drown it;
Think of a plan night and day.
Though I may suffer for this,
I will myself be the king                           50
Of the noble land of Sicily.
I shall labor as well for the downfall
Of the queen, my uncle's wife;
To see that he'll nevermore
Share his life and bed with her.                    55

Then the land will be mine,
If only I can manage that.


[In Damascus]

*Master Platus*
Where are you high-born King,
Mighty lord of Damascus?
My heart is heavy with sorrow                    60
For the things that I have seen.


*The King of Damascus*
Master Platus, what has happened
That has you so dismayed?


*Platus*
Sir King, last night at matins
I was outside in the field                        65
And looking at the firmament.
By the planets in the sky
I saw the birth—in Christendom—
Of a worthy, noble child,
Who will kill you with his sword.                 70
Sir King, he'll take your life
And marry your own daughter
And she will be a Christian.


*King of Damascus*
Master, now do tell me,
When and where was this child born?               75


*Platus*
Sir King, I will tell you that:
Last night the child was born;

His father is the high king
Of Sicily, in Christian lands.

*King of Damascus*
Now Master, answer me this:                                    80
Does this have to be?

*Platus*
My King, yes, by Apollo;
Unless a stronger fate steps in.
But if you will work wisely,
I shall provide a plan                                         85
How and in what manner
You'll remain in your condition;
For good, intelligent counsel
Should here be devised.

*King of Damascus*
Alas, now I'm dismayed                                         90
About these things that you tell me.
My heart is so disconcerted
That I do not know what to do.
But you are such a wise man,
Master Platus, dear friend,                                    95
You've given me long and loyal service
As well as much wise counsel,
So that I've always been honored.
Now I pray you, faithful Master,
That you will help me quickly                                 100
To find a solution,
Let me stay in my current state
Without injury from this youth

That you tell me so much about,
So I may escape him.                                  105

*Platus*
Sir King, lend me your ear,
Noble baron and hero,
And give me, this very moment,
A treasure to take with me;
And I'll ride without delay                           110
To where he can be found.
With my tricks I'll obtain
The noble royal child;
I'll beg Mohammed's help
To get him honestly.                                  115
I shall never return to you
Without bringing him into your power.
Therefore you must give me silver
And gold, Sir King, to spend;
I'll steal him, or buy him for money,                 120
Or get hold of him with some ruse.
That is the advice I give you.
Then he'll be in your power
And become a good paynim.
We'll instruct him after our law                      125
And thus you'll keep your honor;
He'll think you are his father.
Now quickly, for the time is nigh;
I'll go there in great haste.

*King of Damascus*
Master Platus, that's good advice;                    130
Go to that place in haste,
Spare nothing in this effort,

Take treasure enough to spend,
Just take it, without counting,
And bring the young man to me;                    135
Above all I beg you this,
And spare no expense for it,
For I have great desire
To see this young man myself.

*Platus*
Sir King, I promise you truly,                    140
I'll work for this day and night.

## [In Sicily]

*Robert*
Truly, I have waited so long
And now I've obtained my desire.
This child that is so valued
By the old greybeard, my uncle,                   145
And his mother, who love him so—
They never saw a handsomer child.
I'll rob them of this joy
For it gives pain to my heart.
Curses I call on you                              150
And on those who brought you into the world,
For never since, day or night,
Have I felt joy in my heart.
Let them lose their minds over this:
You are at the end of your life,                  155
I'll smother you in a well,
Or make you die even worse a death.

*Platus*
O friend, 't would be a great pity—
He seems a handsome boy.

You're completely out of your mind                    160
If you want to kill this child,
But I see you're very angry,
I can hear from your carrying on.
Pray, tell me your situation—
Why are you so incensed?                              165

*Robert*
Friend, when this child was born
And appeared in this world,
It occurred to me in my sleep
That he would take my life.
I have remained in such worry                         170
That I could not find any rest.
I waited for hours and then
I stole him from his mother;
I plan to end his life
Before he escapes from me.                            175

*Platus*
Friend, if you will listen to me
I'll give you better advice.
Tell me what is his descent,
I pray you by Apollo;
His parentage might be such                           180
That I'd buy him without delay
And take him out of this land
Into pagan land, I assure you,
To a town by the name of Bagdad,
That's way beyond Turkey.                             185

*Robert*
Friend, if you will in fact
Buy the child, then I'll tell you

Who bore him, by whom begot;
I will tell you all of that.
The King of Sicily is his father,                                    190
Highly born, a noble warrior,
And his mother, you should know,
Is the King of Hungary's daughter.

*Platus*
Friend, if that's his descent,
Then he is just what I want;                                         195
If you agree, I will buy him.
Now tell me, what's your price?

*Robert*
For a thousand pounds of gold, friend,
All counted out, you can have him.

*Platus*
Please, friend, here is the gold;                                    200
Now give the boy to me.
But tell me one more thing:
Let me know what his name is.

*Robert*
Esmoreit is his name;
That's what they call the young hero.                                205

*Platus*
Then you can rest assured:
He'll be a pagan forever.
May Mohammed preserve me!
And I'll leave with my guest.

*Robert*
By my faith, now I'm relieved　　　　　　　　210
From the worry that I had.
Forever he'll be hidden
In pagan lands, I know,
For the great town of Bagdad
Is far away, beyond Turkey.　　　　　　　　215
May God's curse be on him:
He alarmed me so much.
Now I will secretly go and
Put the gold in a hiding place,
For it is fine, pure gold.　　　　　　　　　220
If the land never came to me
I would nonetheless still be
A great lord with this money.
I really did very well here,
For the land will be mine too.　　　　　　　225

*[Back in Damascus]*

*Platus*
Where are you noble warrior,
Powerful King of Damascus?
Come here and see the young boy
Who is born of noble blood.

*King of Damascus*
I never felt so relieved　　　　　　　　　230
As now with this great gift.
I'll bring him up as my child
And entrust him to my daughter.

*Platus*

Be sure, Sir King, to hide
From your daughter altogether                               235
Who his mother and his father are.
Don't tell her about that at all,
For you might well regret it;
Sooner or later you would,
Because women are tenderhearted.                           240
If you told her about his high birth
And Venus acted on her,
So she would love the young man,
She might proceed to tell him
How he came to be here.                                    245
For the flame of love, Sir King,
Could blaze up in your daughter
When he is grown up.
Therefore don't tell her a thing
Except that he is a foundling;                              250
The less she will care about him.

*King of Damascus*

Platus, Platus, by Tervagant,
I think you are right in that,
Let this business be forever
Hidden from my daughter;                                   255
Then I'll be at ease about it.
Where are you daughter Damiet?
Come to me without delay,
By Mohammed, I must speak to you.

*Damiet*

I'll be glad to do that, father,                           260
Tell me what is your command.

*King of Damascus*
Damiet, daughter, by God,
Look at this rosy face!
This little boy is a foundling,
Mohammed gave him to me.                                        265
I went walking in the garden,
There I heard him when he was crying,
And there I found this young boy
Under a cedar tree.
Take care of him, Damiet,                                       270
Bring him up as your brother,
Be his sister and his mother;
The boy's name is Esmoreit.

*Damiet*
Lord father, by Tervagant,
I never saw a handsomer child.                                  275
If Mohammed sent us this,
I will thank him and Apollo;
I'll gladly be sister and mother.
O most beloved creature,
You are the most handsome child                                 280
That I ever saw with my eyes.
I should rightly thank Mohammed
That now I'll have a brother;
I'll be his sister and mother.
O Esmoreit, handsome boy,                                       285
How I wonder on this thought:
You were found without protection,
Yet you seem to be nobly born
From the clothing that you wear.
Now come with me, handsome boy,                                 290
I'll treat you as my brother.

## [In Sicily]

*The Christian King*
Where are you, nephew Robert,
Come here, I must speak to you.
I think my heart will break
From the sorrow that I feel.                                295

*Robert*
O dear uncle, noble King,
Why are you so dismayed?

*The Christian King*
I am so tormented with sorrow
That I fear my heart will break.
I've lost my lovely child,                                  300
Esmoreit, my son.
I could not feel more sorrow,
Had I lost in this same way
My riches and my kingdom.
Not a bit I'd mourn for those                               305
If I still had my sweet child.
Alas, alas, bitter grief
I suffer and so does the Queen;
I fear it will cost me my life,
Or my wife's, the noble lady,                               310
So great is her heart's sorrow.
I would rather be dead, I think,
Than suffer this torment.

*Robert*
Alas, esteemed and noble uncle,
Do not wail and lament like this.                           315
I know just what has happened:

My aunt may show great mourning
But she suffers no pain from this;
I've known that all along.
She is full of hate towards you                                    320
Because you are an old man.
I often heard her complaining
When she didn't know I was there.
I often feared that, by ruse,
She'd contrive to take your life.                                  325
She will surely poison you yet;
I've known that all along.
I've often heard her talk
In secret places and moments,
But I never mentioned it                                           330
Before this very hour.
I know she's put the child
To death all by herself.
She never cared much for you
Because your beard is grey.                                        335
She has some other plan
And probably loves a young man.

*The Christian King*
By the father who begot me,
Nephew Robert, if I had known that,
Neither prayer nor treasure would help her!                        340
I would kill that evil woman.

*Robert*
I stake my life on this, uncle:
What I tell you is the truth.
For many years I've known that
She feels no love towards you.                                     345

*The Christian King*
O, how have I deserved this!
Good reason have I to complain!
I thought I saw an angel
When I saw her lovely person,
And now she is so cruel!                                    350
O nephew, I marvel at that.
Now go and bring her here;
I must certainly hear what she says.

*Robert*
Where are you, noble Lady?
Come to the King my uncle.                                  355
Take great care with him, Lady,
He's all beside himself.

*The Lady*
Alas, noble Lord and King,
Who can help us in our wailing
To bear our bitter mourning                                 360
That we have lost our child.

*The Christian King*
Be silent and may God damn you,
Vile whore and evil woman!
All this pain and sorrow
Is brought to me by you                                     365
And you'll pay the price for this.
For I have heard it all,
How this has come about:
You alone committed this murder;
You killed my handsome child                                370
And you'll pay for it with your life.

You are the most evil woman
That ever was born into this world.

*The Lady*
O noble Lord, noble King,
How could I have the heart                                    375
To do any harm to my child
That I carried under my heart?

*The Christian King*
Be silent, bad woman, that's enough!
I won't hear you speak any more:
In a pit I'll have you smothered;                            380
Lead her into prison, Robert.

*The Lady*
God, who was nailed on the cross,
Must now protect and free me,
Bring my innocence to light,
For I know nothing of this.                                  385

*Robert*
Certainly, Lady, it pains me.

*The Lady*
O God, have mercy on me in this torment
That I'm in; I have lost my child,
And they accuse me of the deed.
Mighty God, on whom all depends,                             390
Undeserving and without guilt
You were nailed up on a tree
With three nails, God of meekness.
I pray to you, merciful God,

That the truth will be perceived                               395
And my innocence revealed.
I pray this to you, Queen of Heaven.
Shall I not lose my mind?
That would be a great marvel.
Alas God, who poured this venom                                400
So bitterly over me?
O God, all truth and justice
Come flowing out of you,
Help me now and bring me justice
That my innocence be found.                                    405

### [In Damascus, eighteen years later]

*Young Man*

O Tervagant and Apollo,
How chaste she is, my sister,
And the life that she leads.
In all pagan lands she loves
No man and knows no one                                        410
That she would have for a husband.
By my God Tervagant,
She has such a noble nature,
Or perhaps she loves someone
In secret, that I don't know;                                  415
For she shows no inclination
Toward any man now alive.
I think Mohammed gave her
This noble nature she has.
This is my dear sister's garden,                               420
Where she often walks about.
By my God Apollo,
I too will take my delight here.

Drowsiness comes upon me
I'll rest and sleep here now. 425

*Damiet*
Alas, how great a burden
I carry in my heart.
Overcome I am with a strong love
That I've hidden in my heart.
I complain to you, O Apollo, 430
So strongly do I love this man,
But yet I do not know
His birth or his lineage.
The power of love does this,
It has me caught in its fetters, 435
Alas, since my father found
And brought the child to me
And gave him to me for a foundling,
To be his sister and mother;
Now he thinks he is my brother, 440
But we are not at all related.
Yet I have come to love him
Above all other creatures.
So noble is his nature,
So high in aspiration, 445
He is surely of noble blood,
Even though he was left a foundling.
My heart tells me, inside,
That he is highly born.
O Esmoreit, my beloved, 450
Noble and virtuous hero,
Since my dear father found you,
Now eighteen years ago
Exactly, as I know,

You have been my beloved,                                    455
My brave and excellent hero!
Forever I'll feel this sorrow
For I don't want to tell you—
If I did my father would kill me.

*Young Man*
O my dearest noble lady                                      460
Am I then a foundling?
I fancied that the King
Might have been my father
And you my sister; I thought
That we were closely related.                                465
Alas, now I'm sad in my heart;
By my God Tervagant,
I am the most sorrowful man
That ever was born in this world.
Alas, I am a foundling!                                      470
On this earth no one is sadder;
I thought I was nobly born,
But now it seems I'm a foundling.
By your sweet red mouth I pray you
That you tell me all                                         475
From beginning to end, and uncover
How your father found me.

*Damiet*
O Esmoreit, handsome hero,
Now I am as sad as you are;
I didn't know you were so near                               480
When I told this sad tale.
Noble hero, don't take it badly:
It came from my great love.

*Young Man*

Noble lady, do tell me now
How this has come about.                                      485
I always called you 'dear sister'
But now I have to change that;
I must learn a different tune,
Noble lady, to speak to you
As if I were a stranger.                                          490
But still I must always be
Your friend, and loyal to you
Over all women born on earth.
Noble lady, let me hear
And tell me where I was found.                        495

*Damiet*

O noble youth of high birth,
Now that you have heard me
I will tell you further
Where my father found you—
In his garden, handsome hero,                          500
Where he had gone walking.

*Young Man*

Noble lady, tell me one thing:
Did you never hear people speak,
Ladies or women complaining
That someone had lost a child?                          505

*Damiet*

O dearest, noble youth,
I never heard of that.

*Young Man*

Then I must be of low birth,
I fear, or from far away.
May Mamet allow me to overcome                        510
That scandal, that I may know
Who caused me this shame,
That I was left a foundling.
I will not wait from one night
To the next until I find                              515
From what family I am descended,
And who my father might be.

*Damiet*

O Esmoreit, stay with me,
I pray you, for the sake of all women.
Were my father to die I would                         520
Take you for my husband,
Esmoreit, then you could be
The mighty lord of Damascus.

*Young Man*

Noble lady, that dishonor
Should never happen to you!                            525
That scandal should be far from you
That you'd marry a mere foundling;
Your father is the high King
And you have such great beauty,
You deserve to wear the crown                          530
Before any man now alive.
My heart trembles with shame
That I have come to this.

*Damiet*

O Esmoreit, leave your wailing,
I pray you, noble hero,                                    535
Even if my father would find out
There would be no reproaches.
In great joy without measure
Together we'll live, you and I.

*Young Man*

O noble lady, I will be                                    540
Forever singing your praise,
But never will I delight
In any woman now living,
That can be found on earth,
Till I've found, by Tervagant,                             545
The father who begot me
As well as the mother who bore me.
For the sake of your rosy lips
I have dawdled enough, now I'll go.

*Damiet*

Alas, now I may well be wailing!                           550
I'm all alone in my sorrow;
It's no use talking too much,
I've found that out myself.
Too much talk has oftentimes
Caused much pain and sorrow                                555
And many were lost by babbling.
If only I had remained quiet,
I could have been living in joy
With Esmoreit all my life.
By speaking I chased him away;                             560

'Tis right I should cry 'Alas,'
Alas, that I didn't keep silent
When I spoke those painful words.

*Young Man*
Noble lady, now I will go.
May Mamet preserve your chaste person.                    565
Now I pray you noble lady
Greet my lord, the King, for me
For I shall never return
Unless I have found my lineage
And the person who brought me here,                        570
Where I was left a foundling.

*Damiet*
O handsome young man Esmoreit,
Most meekly I pray you:
When you've learned your condition
Return again to me.                                        575

*Young Man*
O noble heart, lovely lady,
I will certainly not fail to do so.
Directly I shall come back
To find you here, noble lady,
When I have found the truth;                               580
I swear it by Tervagant.

*Damiet*
O Esmoreit, take this cloth:
You were wrapped in it when you
Were found, dear Esmoreit.
Noble youth, I assure you                                  585

If you wind it around your head
And wear it thus in public,
Perhaps someone will see it
And know you by that token.
Remember me, sweet man;           590
I remain here in great sorrow.


*Young Man*
My God, to whom nothing is hidden,
Must now be my consolation.
O Mamet and Apollo,
Mahoen and Tervagant,          595
If the blazons on this cloth
Rightly belong to me,
Then I would feel assured
That I am nobly born;
At least it seems so to me,          600
Because I was wrapped in this
When I was found as a foundling.
That must be my lineage,
My heart assures me of that,
Because I lay wrapped in this.         605
Never more will I be joyful
Unless I have found my lineage
And whoever it was who made me a foundling:
I'll pay him back, by Apollo!
Could I see my mother and father,         610
My heart would be cheered,
And were they of noble birth,
I would be free from all sorrow.

*[During this speech Esmoreit has come to Sicily]*

*The Lady*
Noble youth, come here to me
And speak to me a word;                                615
I heard you in the distance
Bewailing your distress.

*Young Man*
Fair lady, what has happened
That you're imprisoned here?

*The Lady*
Noble youth with your brave heart,                     620
I must be imprisoned like this,
Though I have not done any wrong;
Traitors have done this to me.
Handsome boy, now please tell me:
How did you come to this land                          625
And who gave you that cloth?
Answer me please, handsome youth.

*Young Man*
By my god Mamet, lady,
I'll not refuse you that.
We may well speak of our sorrow                         630
To each other, for you are in prison
And I am much afflicted,
Abandoned as a foundling,
And, truth to say, this cloth
Was wrapped around me then,                             635
Dear lady, when they found me.
Thus publicly I wear it,
In case there might be someone
Who would know me by that.

*The Lady*
Now tell me, handsome youth,                           640
Do you know where you were found?

*Young Man*
Dear lady, in a garden
In Damascus, it's the truth,
The king did find me there
And he has brought me up.                               645

*The Lady*
O God, author of all good,
Blessed be his name.
My heart is filled with joy
That I've lived to see this day
That I now see my child.                                650
My heart could well break with joy:
I see my child, hear him speak,
For whom I suffered such torment.
Welcome my dear child!
Esmoreit, I am your mother                              655
And you my child, you should know.
With my own hands I made
This swaddling band, Esmoreit,
In which you were wrapped,
Esmoreit, when you were found                           660
And when you were taken from me.

*Young Man*
Dear mother, tell me at once:
Who's the father who begot me?

*The Lady*

He is the High King of Sicily;
He is your father, handsome youth.                665
And the King of Hungary,
He is my dear father.
You could not be higher born
In Christendom, far or near.

*Young Man*

Dear mother, tell me now:                        670
Why are you thus imprisoned?

*The Lady*

My dear child, that's because
Of a false and evil traitor;
In your father's ear he whispered
That I had smothered you.                         675

*Young Man*

Alas, what wretched villainy!
He who made the king believe this,
Also brought this sorrow onto me
That I was left a foundling.
O, if I found the truth                           680
And knew who did this deed,
He would be killed for that,
By my God Apollo.
O dear, dear mother mine,
I will not wait any longer                        685
But shorten here your sorrow.
To my father, the high baron,
My first request will be
To bring you out of this prison.

Thanks be to Mamet and Apollo,                                                690
And the creator who made me
That I have found my lineage
And the mother who bore me.
My heart rejoiced with good reason
When I looked at my mother.                                                   695

*The Lady*
Merciful God, thanks must be
Given to you for all times.
I have found my dear child
And he will deliver me.
Without measure is the joy                                                    700
That my heart now feels.

> *[Esmoreit has gone off to speak to his father, but there is*
> *no actual scene of confrontation]*

*Robert* [Aside]
A thief who will be executed,
Alas, would not be as dejected
As I now am in my heart—
I fear great shame and dishonor.                                             705
Had I killed him with my own hands
When I sold him, he would be dead.
Alas, I am much afraid
That harm will come from this.
I will be lost if it comes out                                               710
That I sold him to the Saracen.

*The Christian King*
Go from here, nephew Robert,
And go to my lady, the Queen,
Whom I must love forever

And to whom I owe obedience.                    715
I have kept her imprisoned
Without cause and without guilt.
My heart has much regret
That I was so harsh to her.
Go and get her without delay                    720
And show her this handsome child.

*Robert*
Sir King, most loyally,
Most willingly I'll go.
Noble lady, come out of this prison
Where you have lain so long!                     725
You will behold the young prince
Esmoreit, the young man;
My heart rejoiced inside me
When I saw the handsome hero.

*The Christian King*
Noble lady, give me your hand                    730
And forgive me the wrong that I did.
All my lifetime forever
I will remain your servant,
For the error is all mine—
I have perceived that clearly.                   735
Our child Esmoreit has come here,
A handsome, full-grown youth.
I pray you, by God who has died
For the love of us, forgive me.

*The Lady*
Noble and mighty lord,                           740
Most willingly I forgive you:

All my sorrow is left behind,
All my pain and my distress.
Where is my dear child Esmoreit?
Call him forth and let me see him.                    745

*Robert*
Noble lady, that will be done.
Where are you, cousin Esmoreit?

*Young Man*
I am here, by Apollo.
May Mamet and Mahoen,
Dear father, worthy King,                              750
Give you now a happy day,
And my mother, as well, whom I
Never saw before this time.
I am free of all the sorrow
That I had in my heart                                 755
When I heard that I was a foundling;
I was the most sorrowful man
That ever lived in this world,
But all has turned for the best now.

*The Christian King*
O Esmoreit, let me know,                               760
And tell me this, where did you live?

*Young Man*
With a king who wears his crown
In Damascus, my lord father.
He is a noble Saracen
Who found me in his garden.                            765
And he has a noble daughter

Who received me joyfully
When the king her father found me;
Then she became my mother
And brought me up as her brother—                    770
For this I must ever love her.
She told me everything:
How her father found me,
And that I was wrapped in this cloth
When her father brought me to her.                    775

*The Lady*
This is the cloth that I made,
Esmoreit, handsome man,
I embroidered your father's blazon—
You can see it in three places—
And also the arms of Hungary                           780
Because your descent is from there.
So especially did I love you
That I made it in your honor,
But all that turned to sorrow,
My Esmoreit, when I lost you.                          785
I pray God, who chose the cross,
That he will truly forgive him
Who inflicted this bitter life
That I lived for so long.

*Young Man*
O dear mother, by Apollo,                              790
There was never misdeed or crime
That didn't come out in the end
And receive its own reward.

*Robert*
By the Lord who was crowned
With a crown of thorns,                                    795
Esmoreit, my cousin,
If I knew who had done this
He would be killed for that;
Unless he vanished in the earth,
I would certainly take his life,                          800
Kill him with my sword!
Alas, if I knew that villain
Who brought to you this shame,
In all Christendom he would not
Escape me, but surely die.                                805

*The Lady*
Now we will live in great joy
And forget all our distress,
For my heart is overcome
With joy without measure.

*The Christian King*
My son Esmoreit, let us go                                810
And live in joy together;
But Mamet and Apollin—
These gods you must forsake
And now believe in Mary
And in God, our highest father                            815
Who made us all together:
All that lives in this world
He has made with his art;
The sun and the moon, day and night,
He made them all with his might,                          820
And also the sky and the earth,

Leaves and grass and all such things;
You must believe in this all.

*Young Man*
Father, I pray Him then,
The high God on His throne,                                    825
That He will protect Damiet,
The fair one, above all that lives
For she has brought me up;
Therefore I must truly love her,
The young queen of Damascus,                                   830
Damiet, the noble lady.
O God, preserve her chaste person
For she is noble and good;
Most surely I must love her
Above all alive on this earth;                                 835
If I did not, I would be wrong
For she is the love of my heart.

*Robert*
Esmoreit, cousin, she deserves it.
Now we will forget all sorrow
And in good cheer go to dinner                                 840
For the table is all prepared.

                      *[In Damascus]*
*Damiet*
Alas, where could dear Esmoreit
Linger that he does not return?
I fear that he is lost
Or has died an evil death,                                     845
Unless he is in such great joy
That he has forgotten me.

But I will know the truth,
How his situation is,
Though I may have to go to the end of the world.          850
Where are you Platus, wise Master?

*Platus*
Noble Lady, faithful and good,
To your service I am prepared.

*Damiet*
Master, I want to go now
To look for Esmoreit throughout the lands.          855
Though I might suffer shame,
Hunger, thirst and adversity,
This will just have to be;
Honest love forces me to this.
Dear Master, I pray you now          860
That you don't deny me this,
But stay with me and counsel me
How we may be able to find him.

*Platus*
Lady, be in good spirits!
Since it is your desire,          865
And you esteem the young man so highly,
We will search for the noble lord.

*Damiet*
Master Platus, let us go then
As if we were two pilgrims.
"Isn't there someone here          870
Who will give something to us,

Two pilgrims who have been exiled
And robbed by violent thieves?"

*[During these lines Damiet and Platus have arrived in Sicily]*
*Young Man*
O there I hear Damiet
If ever I heard her before.                                    875
O worthy Virgin Saint Mary,
How much she speaks just like her,
Damiet, my fair beloved,
The beautiful queen of Damascus
Whom I love above all women                                    880
That are born here on earth!
Now speak and let me hear you,
You speak so much like her.

*Damiet*
Were I in the realm of Damascus,
Esmoreit, handsome man,                                        885
I would be even more like her.
But now I stand here as a pilgrim.

*Young Man*
O my dear lady Damiet,
Is it really you, noble lady?
My heart, my soul and my body                                  890
Now may truly live in joy
For I never saw dearer friend
Who was ever born on this earth.
O let me hear, noble lady,
How you have come to this land?                                895

*Damiet*

O Esmoreit, handsome hero,
I thought of you and wanted
To see you, but I could not
And I suffered grief for that.
Then I disguised myself as a pilgrim                            900
And came wandering through the land
And took Platus by the hand,
That he would be my protector.

*Young Man*

Where are you, my dear father?
Come here, and you will see her                                 905
Whose heart is attached
In loyal love to me.
I owe it to her to love her,
She's done so much for me.

*The Christian King*

Then I'll greet her with joyful heart.                          910
Welcome, lovely Damiet,
You will wear the crown in Sicily
Over all who live there.
I will pass it on to my son
And you'll surely be his wife                                   915
For I am so old and tired
That I can't wear it any more.

*Robert*

By Saint John, Sir King and uncle,
Esmoreit is worthy of this.
He'll be a knight of great renown                               920
And carry weapons valiantly.

This plan seems well devised
That he'll receive the crown from you.
Now Damiet, follow the king:
You will be the young queen.                                925

*Platus*

Help me, Mamet, I can't believe
That I'm not going out of my mind!
O Esmoreit, noble knight,
This man brought you to this sorrow.
He doesn't mean what he tells you,                         930
He is totally false to you!
I bought you from him for fine gold;
A thousand pounds I gave him.

*Young Man*

Master, now tell me this:
How does this matter stand?                                 935

*Platus*

O Esmoreit, by Apollo,
It is now eighteen years ago
That I came riding here,
To this same spot, Esmoreit.
Now hear what the villain did—                             940
He would surely have smothered you!
He spoke such violent words:
That you'd rob him of his realm.
You must be related to him—
I could tell from his carrying on.                          945

*Young Man*

I beg you most urgently, Master,
To tell me the whole affair,

For I am quite bewildered
Because I don't know the truth.
Who did this great harm to my mother 950
And brought me so much shame?

*Platus*
O Esmoreit, by Mohammed,
This same man did it all!
By my God Tervagant,
He would have taken your life— 955
That was his plan, the villain,
I heard him, and I spoke to him
And said it would be wrong
To murder this young prince.
And then I bought you from him 960
For a thousand pounds of red gold.

*Young Man*
By the Lord who has redeemed me,
This crime shall be avenged
Before I eat or drink wine.
Today shall be your last day! 965
Where are you, high lord, my father?
And you, Robert, murderer?

*Robert*
By the Lord, this is not true!
Esmoreit my cousin,
I have always been good and loyal, 970
Never murderer or traitor.

*Young Man*
Be quiet, whore's son, it is worse yet,
This misdeed that you have done!

How did it enter your mind
To sell your own flesh and blood                              975
And to make my father believe
That my mother had done this thing?

*Robert*
I will go to battle for this,
Esmoreit, bold-hearted hero;
Is there anyone in the land                                  980
Who wants to accuse me of this?

*Platus*
Be silent, you miscreant,
You would have stabbed him to death
If you had not heard me speak,
When I suddenly appeared!                                    985
I was never so satisfied
As when I bought him from you;
I gave you the gold without counting
In a handsome ivory box;
We might find it in your closet,                             990
I bet my life on that.

*Young Man*
Alas Robert, cruel villain,
You really deserve all my hate;
This will be your day of Judgement,
All the world can help you no more.                          995

*[Here they hang Robert.]*

*Young Man once more*
It has happened many times:

Evil deeds come to evil reward,
But pure hearts carry the palm,
For they are virtuous and loyal.
So I counsel you, ladies and gentlemen, 1000
To direct your heart to virtue
So you'll end up united with God
Up there in the high heavens
Where the angels are singing sweetly.
May the heavenly Father grant it 1005
And say Amen all together.

*Amen xc.viii verses*[1]

*Platus*
May God take us all in protection!
Now you wise and sensible people,
Listen here and understand
How Esmoreit took his vengeance 1010
On Robert his cousin, right here.
Stay quietly in your seats,
Let no one wish to go home.
We will play you now a farce
That will be short, I assure you. 1015
If you're hungry, go and eat,
And go down the steps.
If you wish, you can come back tomorrow.

---

[1]Throughout the manuscript, the number of lines in the play is listed at the end of each text. In this case, Platus' epilogue must have been added later, as was the epilogue to *Lippin*.

# LIPPIN

## The Characters

Lippin
His Wife
Her Lover
The Gossip

# Here Begins the Farce

*Here begins the Wife*
Well well, and God help me!
I will go and have some fun
With my sweetheart in the field.
It's a long time since I saw him!
Say, Lippin, where are you?                                    5

*Lippin*
I am here, what do you want?

*His Wife*
Go Lippin, fetch water and fire;
I'll return here very soon
And bring us something to eat.

*Lippin*
By God's death, you will forget—                               10
You always stay so long!

*His Wife*
Well, Lippin, don't be annoyed:
I always have so much to do!
By the time I've been to mass
It is already mid-day.                                          15
And before I get to the butcher—
If I want to get a good bargain—
I must wait until the crowd
Has gone away from there.
That's why I must stay so long,                                20
Dear Lippin, you must know that.

*Lippin*
Well, truly, tell me another,
And I don't know what to say.
Go on and I'll make the fire,
Fetch water and scour the pot,                                     25
For truly, so help me God,
I have made myself your slave.

*His Wife*
Lippin dear, wash the dishes too
And sweep the floor all clean.

*Lippin*
Listen dear, may God reward you!                                   30
And don't stay away too long.
All my days I've been your poor slave
And I will be all my life.

*His Wife* [aside]
Shut up, may God give you shame,
You're living too long for my taste.                               35
                    *[Moves aside or outside]*
Now was this not a smart trick?
Where are you, friend of my heart?
He will end up on the gallows
For making me wait like this!

*Her Lover*
All manner of things have kept me,                                 40
My love, did you wait here long?

*Lippin's Wife*
Yes, I have, and I'm pretty sad
That I haven't seen you for so long.

*Her Lover*
Let us drink and have a good time now,
Most beloved, dear sweetheart,                          45
We'll be happy till nighttime,
Come on, snuggle up to me.

     *[Somehow Lippin has discovered his wife and her lover]*
*Lippin*
Alas, Lord, can this be true?
By God, I have seen enough!
She lies there with her bare knees                       50
And he has crept in between.
God's death, he has snuck in there.
Look at this whore, and she tells me
That she goes to mass every day!
There she rolls around with another                      55
And puts the horns on poor me.
She says she goes to the butcher's!
But by Saint John, I'll fix her,
Get even with her before night-time.
If I can find a good stick                                60
I'll tan her hide so badly
That she'll regret this game
That she has played with him!

*The Gossip*
Hey Lippin, God give you good day,
How are you; what's going on?                             65

*Lippin*
Oh, Trise, my heart is breaking,
For the pain that I feel:
I would never have expected
That my wife would do such a thing.

*The Gossip*
Lippin, now let me know:                                    70
How and in what way?

*Lippin*
I must be ashamed forever:
She rolls around with another man.

*The Gossip*
Truly, I can't believe that—
Not of your wife, for sure.                                 75
I know her, she is chaste-living,
She'd not do that for all the world.

*Lippin*
When a man sees it with his own eyes
It's hard to persuade him otherwise.

*The Gossip*
May I live in honor, Lippin,                                80
Many men were fooled by their eyes.

*Lippin*
No way, this is no lying:
I saw it with my own eyes—
She was naked up to her knees
And they were both carrying on.                             85

*The Gossip*

O Lippin, you shouldn't say that,
'Twould bring scandal to your wife.
Your eyes are all disturbed
With drinking and old age!
Good Lippin, don't talk about it:                    90
It would bring shame on your wife.


*Lippin*

What the devil, are you making me blind?
When I saw it with my own eyes?
I saw her lie on her back
And he picked up her skirts.                          95


*The Gossip*

Please be still now, good Lippin,
It was all in your own mind—
You never heard of apparitions?
How they often fool the people?
The devil doesn't mind one lie                       100
To make trouble between man and wife.
I will stake my life on this:
That it was a ghost that you saw.


*Lippin*

What the devil, even if God afflicts us
With ghostly apparitions—                            105
Wouldn't I still know my own wife?
That would be a perilous thing.
I saw her go off with him
And he pulled her close in his arms.

*The Gossip*
Lippin, such lies were never true; 110
I know your wife too well,
She is so chaste and modest,
She'd not do it for a world of gold.
But elves can do anything;
They can make a man so blind 115
He no longer knows himself—
So how can he know another?

*Lippin*
By God's death, you're driving me crazy,
What the devil has happened to me?
Am I blind, can I not see? 120
I never saw such marvelous things;

*[He gestures towards the audience]*
And yet I can see all these people,
Sitting here all around!
So truly I cannot be blind
As you'd like me to believe. 125

*The Gossip*
Lippin, do you know what you're doing?
I beg you don't say it again,
But treat your wife with respect—
It's a ghost that torments you;
She's upset your eyesight completely. 130
Your eyes are all out of joint.

*Lippin*
Dear me, is that what ails me?
I really thought it was her.

*The Gossip*
'Twas an elf that was lying there,
I swear it to you by the cross.                                    135
Your wife is still in the house,
I bet you a beer on that.

*Lippin*
She told me to fetch fire and water,
And she would get us some food.

*The Gossip*
Well, Lippin, you want to know the truth?          140
You were altogether misled!
An elf has spread her nets
To catch you, I can see that.
Come with me, we'll go to your door
And your wife will be sitting by the fire.               145

*Lippin*
What, could I be drunk with beer
Or do elves fly by the roads?

*The Gossip* [knocks on the door]
Hey, friend, won't you let us in?

*Lippin's Wife*
Jeez knows, sure, who is there?

*The Gossip*
Well, Lippin, did I tell you the truth?                   150

*Lippin*
Praised be God in heaven,
I never saw such a thing!
I can see it is all my fault.

*The Gossip*
What did I say, Lippin dear?
But you wouldn't listen to me.                    155
My friend is faithful and true,
But you make her out for a whore.

*The Wife*
God give him cramp in his jaws—
Did he accuse me of that?

*The Gossip*
Yes, he said you slept with another;              160
He complained to me about that.

*Lippin*
I really thought that I saw it,
But I am satisfied now.
Trise can explain it all right
But, as if I were there myself                     165
I thought you got up in the morning
And told me to fetch fire and water . . .

*His Wife*
Shut up, you filthy carrion,
You accuse me of doing it with another?

*Lippin*
Well, yes, to tell you the truth,                              170
I saw it, or my eyes deceived me,
But Trise explained it to me:
She says an elf has fooled me.

*His Wife*
So then why did you lie about me
And put me to shame everywhere?                               175

*Lippin*
Well, sweetie, I'll make it up
If I did or said anything wrong.

*His Wife*
But you'll get blows for that, though,
you dirty, nasty old man.

*The Gossip*
By the Lord, he does deserve it                               180
That we walk all over him.

*Lippin*
Dear wife, I'll never say it again;
I didn't know, I was all confused!

*His Wife*
Well, we will teach you a lesson!

*[Here they fight.]*
*Nota c.lxxxiii verses*

*[Epilogue]*

Good people, here we have                                    185
Played a farce for you.
You all know people around
Who have seen such a thing themselves.
Many jokes are played, to be sure,
That they don't talk about like this.                        190
So I pray you that you accept
Our drollery in good spirits,
And I pray the King of Grace,
Who was born of the Virgin,
That no one take offense                                     195
At what he has seen here, and heard.
Get up now, you can leave,
For we all have to go our way.
May our Lord God guide us all.
Amen.

# GLORIANT

## The Characters

Gerald, the Duke's uncle
Geoffrey, a counselor
Red Lion, King of Abelant
Florentine, his daughter
Roger, Florentine's messenger
Florant, the King's nephew
The Hangman

# An *Abel* Play and Noble Tale

# of The Duke of Brunswick

# How He Fell in Love

# With the Daughter of Red Lion of Abelant

## And a Farce to Follow

### [Prologue]

I pray to God the highest father
That he may preserve us all together,
Ladies and gentlemen, high and low.
I pray you all in this company
That you will be silent                                    5
And pay attention all who will.
We will play you an excellent tale
About a noble young man
Who was duke of Brunswick.
He thought that none equal to him                         10
Could be found in this world.
And from his proud thoughts he spoke
Vaunting words without knowledge
Such as often bring men to fall.
For to him who boasts too highly,                         15
When things take a different turn
His boast will bring him to ruin—
And that's what befell this hero.
Though he was mighty and high-born
By his vaunting he came to grief.                         20

Because he spoke boasting words
Lady Venus became vexed with him
And afterwards she took revenge
For the boasting words he spoke;
You will see that here yourself.                                  25
Now I counsel you, lords and ladies,
That no one take too much pride;
It will rarely bring him honor:
Too much pride was never praised.
Now we pray to God who was                                       30
Nailed to the cross for our sins
That we will all be saved
In the sweet valley of Josephat
Where God will sit in judgment;
To Mary our Queen we pray too.                                   35
Now be still and listen; we'll start.

*Gerald, the Duke's Uncle*
Where are you dear friend Geoffrey?

*Geoffrey*
Here I am, Sir Gerald,
Now tell me what is your counsel?

*Gerald*
It wouldn't seem bad to me, Geoffrey,                            40
If the great knight our Duke
Would enter into marriage
And take himself a wife.
He is such a handsome figure,
He is strong and fully of age;                                   45
A wife could bear him children
For the benefit of the land.

It is a large and vast country;
What a shame if there were no descendants!
Therefore I called you here                          50
That you give us counsel in this.

*Geoffrey*
Sir Gerald, 'twould do no harm;
I recently thought the same.
But I tell you without feigning,
Sir Gerald, you are the Duke's uncle:                55
Therefore you must serve his interests
More than I, who am not related.

*Gerald*
Nonetheless, Geoffrey, you may
Counsel us how we must proceed.
The land would rejoice if he had                     60
A wife, and children with her.

*Geoffrey*
Sir Gerald, you and I must together
Pay close attention to this:
One person who would be fitting
—And they'll be glad to give her—                    65
The daughter of the King of Auvergne;[2]
She is a good and noble daughter
And she has a pure heart too,
And her ancestry is good.

---

[2]The manuscript has *Averne*, usually read as "Auvergne." See also *Lancelot of Denmark*, line 461, note 7. For a different view, see Kuiper (1997).

*Gerald*
Certainly, Sir Geoffrey,                                            70
'T would seem a good marriage to me,
The King of Auvergne is a noble man.
In all his days he always bore
His arms in honorable wise
And his ancestors are a noble line.                                75
Certainly, Geoffrey, I think
That marriage would be well done.

*Geoffrey*
Then let us go to the Duke
And present him with this plan.
Then we may hear him say                                           80
What his thoughts on this are.
Now let us go, you and I,
And let us hear what he says;
If his heart is inclined to this
Then we will arrange the marriage.                                 85
Where are you Duke, noble Lord,
High Duke of Brunswick?

*The Duke*
Welcome, uncle, most certainly,
And my dear friend Geoffrey.
Now tell me, dear uncle Gerald,                                    90
What you desire, and it will be done.

*Gerald*
Nephew Gloriant, we would like
To see you joined in marriage;
We would love to see that, noble Baron,
And so would Brunswick, your land.                                 95

*The Duke*
Uncle Gerald, noble hero,
I'm not yet inclined to do that;
I pray you: Do not vex me.
I will not hear a word of that.
There's no woman here on earth                          100
With whom I would spend my life.

*Gerald*
For the sake of the land you must,
Dear nephew, and for yourself too.
You must take yourself a wife,
Nephew, to have children by her.                        105

*Geoffrey*
Now I can no longer stay silent,
Noble Duke and worthy knight;
For the sake of the land you must
Have children, as Gerald says.
It is a thing not commonly done                         110
For a great lord to be without a wife;
You would dishonor your realm,
Noble lord, if you died without heirs.
Great discord would arise from that:
Everyone would be next of kin.                          115
You would bring about great pain
To your noble land of Brunswick.

*The Duke*
Geoffrey, Geoffrey, certainly,
Your words are all in vain.
My heart loves no woman so much                         120
That I would care a straw for her.

I know of no woman so deserving
That I would make her my lady.

*Geoffrey*
My lord, watch out! you'll regret
That you spoke such a stupid word:                    125
Lady Venus will be vexed with you
And she'll cut you down to size.

*Gerald*
Gloriant, nephew, remember
That Samson, who was so strong,
Was betrayed by the force of love;                    130
Also handsome Absalon,
And wise King Solomon, too:
They were all brought down by love.
That's forever true, without lies:
Love for women ruined them all.                       135

*The Duke*
Surely, uncle, I wonder at that;
But they were full of foolishness,
Uncle Gerald of Normandy,
And on top of that there was this:
They did not rule their own hearts;                   140
By women they were all befuddled.
I know no woman so nobly-born
That I'd care two pins for her.

*Gerald*
Surely, nephew, it's a joke
Hearing you talk like that;                            145
And I never heard a mighty man

Speaking such stupid words.
Surely, nephew, you must nonetheless
Marry for the sake of your land.


*The Duke*
Surely, uncle, but that moment                    150
No man shall ever observe,
That I marry any woman
Now living on this earth
Or within this whole world.
For I have such a valiant body,                    155
If I joined it to a woman
I would certainly lose my mind.
Furthermore I am such a great lord
Of the Duchy of Brunswick
That no woman in the world is my equal            160
And I will remain my own man.


*Gerald*
By the father who begot me,
I never heard such foolish words!
Surely, nephew, it does not become you
To speak so ill of women.                          165


*Geoffrey*
Surely, Gerald, you speak the truth.
He has spoken very ill of women,
But it will yet be avenged;
I know that, in all truth.
The sight of a lovely woman                         170
Will come to seem medicine to him.

---

*The Duke*

Uncle Gerald, by my troth,
You will never experience that!
My heart is as steadfast as a bastion,
All set to protect my handsome body.                    175
In this world I know no woman
Who seems to be worthy of me;
My heart soars like the eagle
High above the love of women.
Should I lay my heart, my five senses,                  180
In the power of a woman?
May God's vengeance come upon me
If that would ever happen.

*Gerald*

Nephew Gloriant, it's all in vain,
That I take the trouble, I hear that,                    185
But watch out that you won't regret
That you speak so foolishly!

*[In Abelant]*

*Florentine the Maiden*

Alas, in all this world
My equal has not been born,
Nor one who is similar in nature                         190
Or like to me in spirit.
I never saw a strong, rich man
Whom I would have as a husband,
Neither an emir or a sultan,
Nor other man of high birth,                             195
Who would woo me for a marriage
And whose love I could accept.
I have heard the same complaint

From a man in Christendom—
That is the Duke of Brunswick.                              200
His heart is so courageous
And his spirit so supercilious
That he also loves no woman.
We are of the same inclination!
My heart tells me so for certain:                          205
We are born under one constellation
And we both have the same nature.
Now I will send him a portrait
Made after my appearance.
If we two are really alike,                                 210
Then his heart will change inside.
By my god Tervagant,
I will hear what he pines for.
My heart is devoted to him
Because he's so proud in his heart.                        215
Where are you, Roger, my herald?
Come here, I need you for something.

*Roger*
Noble lady, by Mahoun,
Tell me what you want me to do.

*Florentine*
Roger, you must go hastily                                  220
To the Duke of the land of Brunswick,
It's located in the Christian world,
And his name is Gloriant.
You shall give him, the noble hero,
Into his own hands this portrait,                           225
And tell him that I had it made
After my own likeness

And that you come from the land
And the town of Abelant.
Tell him also, the noble warrior,                           230
That I beg him in good faith
That, in honor of all women,
He observe this portrait.
He will marvel greatly at this,
To know what I have in mind.                                235
Tell him that I never saw man
With whom I would share my life.
And tell him also right away
That my father is the high baron
Of Abelant, named Red Lion.                                 240
Hear, take note, be discreet and silent;
Pay attention to his words,
And bring the message to me.

*Roger*
By my god Tervagant, lady,
This errand will be done;                                    245
I will go there in haste.

*[During this speech Roger travels to Brunswick]*

May Mohammed and Apollo
Preserve my dear lady
Who has sent me over here.
Noble lord, I am a messenger                                 250
Of a noble and virtuous lady;
She prays with true meekness
That you observe this picture
Made after the loveliest creature
That can be found in this world                              255
And so closely like her appearance

As if it were the lady herself.
She is renowned for her virtue
And also for her noble nature.

*The Duke*
Herald, now tell me this:                                    260
Who is this lady, let me know.

*Roger*
She is Florentine of Abelant,
The noble lady and mighty too;
In pagan lands you can't find her equal.
Such a noble and lovely person—                              265
In all the world you can't find five
Equal to my lady herself!
She could not be more noble,
More courteous or more lovely:
So perfect in her body,                                       270
So honorable in her person!
No man has appeared on this earth,
So mighty or so highly born,
Who proposed his love to her
That she would be his wife.                                    275
She is utterly chaste and pure
And her father a man of high standing:
He is the Red Lion of Abelant,
That is her father, you should know.

*The Duke*
You are a good and loyal herald,                              280
I hear that from your words.
Now get up and come with me,
I will see you well provided for.

*Roger*
Gladly I will, noble baron.

*The Duke*
Now I pray to God the Almighty                                              285
That he let me live 'till the day
When I may behold this lady
Who has shown me such affection
And has sent me this portrait,
This picture of her appearance.[3]                                          290
O God, if her appearance
Is really like this portrait,
On this earth I have seen no one like her;
She would well deserve to be
Lady and Duchess of Brunswick.                                             295
May God, master of all virtues,
Bless her every day.
O God, what talents are hidden
In her heart, I can see that well.
She bears the palm of noble graces                                         300
Above all women I ever saw.
May God grant blessings to her
Who has sent me this pledge.

*Roger*
O noble, high-born hero,
I have brought my message to you;                                          305
Now I will return again
To the lady Florentine.

---

[3]The text has *gheprent*, but this is too early a date for a printed portrait. It might be a painted medallion or a carved portrait, like a cameo.

*The Duke*

Roger, Roger, now you must be
Good and loyal at all times
And bear a courteous message.                                      310
What you hear and what you see
You will not pass on further,
Roger, than you are asked to.
'Tis laudable to keep one's counsel!
Dear Roger, now be loyal                                           315
And greet for me the noble lady
And tell her truthfully
That never woman received from me
More greetings than she alone;
But because she is so chaste                                       320
And such an excellent person,
Ask that noble, lovely lady
To preserve her purity for me
To the bliss of both of us,
And I will be constant to her.                                     325

*Roger*

O noble lord, by Apollo
She begged me most urgently
That I would ask you, noble lord,
If she would ever get to see you.

*The Duke*

Roger, that she will:                                              330
Before these seven weeks are past
I will see and speak to the lady,
If God preserve my life.
Now greet the lady fervently
And may God preserve her always.                                   335

*Roger*

Now I will run in great haste

[*Back in Abelant*]

May Mohammed and Apollo
And Mahoen and Jupiter
Grant you a good day.

*Florentine*

Now Roger, report to me:                                340
Have you seen the noble hero?

*Roger*

Yes I have, lady, by Tervagant;
He is a most worthy man.
I know well that on this earth
His equal is not alive,                                 345
And the world contains not his like
In beauty and high-mindedness;
He is a man of noble birth,
Well-endowed, of high descent,
Nobly born and with great power,                        350
And he keeps a splendid court.
I never heard such praise
As was given to Gloriant,
The epitome of a brave hero
And respected by all men.                               355

*Florentine*

Roger, Roger, now tell me
What greetings did he send?

*Roger*

Noble lady of great renown,
He said to me truthfully
That no woman ever received                                    360
Greetings from him such as you.
He prays you, noble, chaste lady,
To preserve your chastity for him,
To the bliss of both of you,
And he'll be constant to you.                                  365

*Florentine*

Tell me, Roger, by Apollo,
Did he say he'd like to see me?

*Roger*

Yes he did, lady, and it will happen:
Before seven weeks have passed
He will see you and speak with you also;                        370
That's what the warrior told me,
And he shook hands on the promise,
And swore to it by his faith.

*Florentine*

By my great God Apollo
I'll look out for that day!                                     375
If it happens, as I expect
It will come to happen to me,
That I see the Duke in person,
I'll be free of all my cares.
Roger, get up and come with me;                                380
You performed your embassy well.

*[In Brunswick]*

*Gloriant*
Where are you, uncle Gerald,
Mighty baron of Normandy?
I am in need of your counsel,
Noble uncle, mighty warrior.                                    385

*Gerald*
What do you say, nephew Gloriant,
What is it that you need?

*Gloriant*
Noble uncle, I cannot conceal
That my heart is pierced through!
True love makes me suffer so                                    390
That it will cost me my life.
I love a noble woman so strongly
That I cannot rest or sleep
For one hour, day or night,
Since I first began to love.                                    395

*Gerald*
This is something that I cannot
Conceive of. How it may happen
That your noble heart suffers pain
For any woman now living
Or within this whole world?                                     400
I can't believe one word of it.

*The Duke*
Noble uncle of wide renown,
I confess and grant myself guilty

That before this time I have
Often spoken stupidly.                                        405
Noble uncle, that's all avenged now
That I spoke those stupid words;
Lady Venus is angry about them
And has struck me in my heart
And made me a servant of ladies                               410
And taught me to walk in step with love.

*Gerald*
And how should I believe that?
You carry yourself so proudly!
You assured me and Geoffrey
That no woman on this earth,                                  415
However highborn and mighty,
Seemed to be worthy of you;
Your heart soared like the eagle
High above the power of love.
This can not enter your mind:                                 420
It's all in jest, what you say;
Your heart is filled with pride;
Women can't get the better of you!

*The Duke*
O noble uncle, understand me:
If I spoke so stupidly                                        425
That was because I was lacking
Any knowledge, truth to tell.
Now I humble myself for all women
Because for one I languish;
For heart and sense, body and passion                        430
Are all in the hands of one lady.

*Gerald*

Who's the lady who torments you,
Nephew Gloriant, tell me that?
For I can still not forget
The proud words that you spoke—                    435
Did you now get caught in love?
Surely, nephew, that's a surprise!
Do tell me who she is,
Who weighs down your heart like this.

*The Duke*

Uncle Gerald of Normandy,                          440
Her name is Florentine of Abelant.
Noble uncle, valiant warrior,
She has a father of high condition.
He is Red Lion of Abelant;
He's her father, you should know.                  445

*Gerald*

Help, Lord God in Paradise,
Nephew, how could that happen?
My heart marvels much at that
Because she lives far from here.

*The Duke*

Noble uncle, the flame of love                     450
Moves faster than any arrow.
Uncle Gerald, by my God,
She has sent me a greeting
And a picture made after her face,
An appearance just like hers.                      455
She is the most beautiful creature
That lives under the stars,

She is worthy to wear the crown
Even from the King of France;
She's not like any other woman                          460
That the sun looks down upon.
My heart is in torment about her;
Truly uncle, she is worthy of that.
She is renowned for her virtue
And for her high-mindedness also.                       465
Noble uncle, I'm telling you this—
My secret, hidden condition—
I pray you uncle, advise me
How I may win my beloved.

*Gerald*
Nephew Gloriant, such a thing                           470
Will never happen to you.
You may well look for another
And I will tell you why:
Red Lion, he is very mighty
And a man of great power                                475
And he hates all our lineage
Above all that live on earth.
For with my sword I killed
His father before Abelant,
And your father, the brave hero,                        480
Killed his uncle Isembart,
The bravest that ever existed
And girt the sword in pagan lands;
But your father of wide renown
Cut his neck in two                                     485
And he caused him even more harm
For which he never smiled again:
He killed his aunt's two sons

That were born in Antioch.
Therefore is Red Lion still angry! 490
I know that for the truth.
Though you were king of all Christendom
He'd not give his daughter to you.

*The Duke*
By God who was nailed on the cross,
Uncle Gerald of Normandy, 495
And by the Virgin Saint Mary,
I'll have her or lose my life!
No matter how great in power
Or in enmity he were,
Wisdom is better than strength. 500
I'll win the lovely lady
In my own person only;
I'll get her if God will permit.

*Gerald*
Gloriant, nephew, stop jesting:
How will you contrive such a thing? 505

*The Duke*
I'll tell you, noble man,
Brave hero of Normandy:
Unknown by all I'll ride there,
Like a knight of adventure.
I must endure the path of love 510
For Florentine, the noble lady.
Noble uncle, now remain loyal
To the good land of Brunswick
For no one equal in valor

To you, noble uncle, is alive.                        515
I pray you, do not forsake us
But be loyal to the good land;
Ward off shame from me all around,
This I pray you, uncle Gerald.
If I were to die on my journey,                       520
Then the land will devolve onto you.
May you be with God, brave hero,
This road must now be traveled.

*Gerald*
O my nephew Gloriant,
I fear you'll regret this journey.                    525
You can find many lovelier women
In Christendom, noble baron.
And Red Lion, he is so fierce;
If he finds out about your lineage,
The marvels that your father wrought                  530
Before Abelant among his men,
He will cause you great harm;
Truly, nephew, that's what I fear.

*The Duke*
Well, come of this what may,
This road must still be taken.                        535

*Gerald*
May it turn out well for you!
For this I pray God in Heaven.
Nephew Gloriant, may God reward you.
Be discerning in your plans;
Do not make to any person                             540
Your secret condition known;

Be a man of fewest words,
And let those be shrewd and firm.
When you reach what your heart longs for—
Florentine the good lady—                                      545
Then carry yourself like a knight
And decidedly not too hasty!
If you get into difficulty,
Then let me know, dear nephew;
I'll certainly be as your father                               550
As long as God keeps me alive;
But if you gave up on this journey
It would be wisely done.

*The Duke*
Not so, uncle, for all the wealth
That sees the light of day                                     555
I will not fail to see her,
Florentine that noble lady.
Where is my horse Valentif?
I will go in great haste.
But noble and loyal good uncle,                                560
My land is in your command.
May you keep it steady and safe
Till I come back from Abelant.

*Gerald*
O noble nephew Gloriant,
May our Lord God preserve you                                  565
And keep you alive and virtuous
Wherever you may turn!

*[During this monologue Gloriant travels to Abelant]*

*The Duke*
Oh God, how does love teach me
Courtliness, as I can see.
My heart was hostile to women                                    570
Till I started to love that beauty,
But now all women rule
In my heart and that is all
Because of lovely Florentine!
She shows me the path of love.                                    575
O mighty God, so love compelled
You to come down from above
And to take on human nature
In a virgin, a virtuous woman.
You took on a human body,                                        580
You let it be hung on a tree,
Undeserved and without blame,
Let your noble heart be struck
By a lance, all pierced through.
All that did the force of love!                                   585
O God, what wonder have you wrought
All from the flood of true love!
Therefore all who know its meaning
Do not need to reproach me
That love gives me great sorrow;                                  590
For love has such strong power
That it caused Almighty God
To descend from heaven
To pay our debt for us.
The nature of love did that,                                      595
Made Him choose the noble garden,

Mary, the noble vessel,
In which was hidden the treasure
That has bought us all free,
Led us out of eternal pain.                                    600
O love, you are a noble plant,
You are the sweetest fruit
That God ever made grow on earth.
Now I see Abelant, the noble city,
Wherein my lady dwells.                                        605
It seems to be locked up—
That's right, it is two in the night;
I'd expect the people to guard it;
Good security makes good peace.[4]
Abelant, Abelant, sweetest town,                              610
Since I may not enter you,
I will wait until the morning
And take my night's rest here.
Valentif will graze in the green
Until the sun rises up.                                        615

*Florentine*
Thanks be to Mohammed and Apollo!
I see the falcon of noble birth
For whom I have waited so long
Coming down into my garden;
He has brought a token before him                             620
By which I recognize him.[5]
He's the one that I love truly,

---

[4] Proverbial; see Jente, *Proverbia communia*, 156, and Johnson, *Walewein*, 6971.

[5] This might be the medallion or cameo with Florentine's portrait, or a blazon with Gloriant's coat of arms.

I see that by his appearance.
Now I will welcome him warmly
For he has come to perch on my hand,                            625
A noble falcon from Christenland,
The high baron from Brunswick.
I saw him dismount from his horse
Onto the grass, the brave hero.
I welcome you, Gloriant,                                        630
You have captured my heart!
I saw you in the moonlight
And I heard you speak as well;
Right away I recognized you
By the token you carry there.                                   635

*The Duke*
O Florentine, lovely maiden,
Is it you, noble pure lady?
To the God from Nazareth I pray
That he protect your chaste person.
O Florentine, lovely woman,                                     640
How I have suffered for you
And hazarded for your sake
Before I came to this land!

*Florentine*
O noble Duke Gloriant,
You are most welcome here!                                      645
You may well pride yourself
That I saw no man on this earth
Who gives my heart more joy
Than you do, noble baron,
But if my father, Red Lion,                                     650
Knew that we are here together,

By my God Apollo,
We'd lose our lives, both of us.

*The Duke*
God, who was born from a maiden,
Must preserve the two of us.                                    655
O my chosen love, Florentine,
Mirror above all women,
Shall it be all in vain
What I have done for your sake?
I have left my lands behind                                      660
To speak to you, chaste lady,
And I come here wandering alone
Just like a common young man.

*Florentine*
O Gloriant, that would be wrong!
By my God Tervagant,                                            665
It is just, when one favors someone
And loves her in good faith
That he wins solace from her;
As I have received from you,
So you shall receive from me                                     670
All that your heart desires
In virtue, worthy knight,
Without any shamefulness.

*The Duke*
By the Virgin Saint Mary,
Most virtuous Florentine,                                        675
For all the goods on this earth
I'd do nothing shameful to you!
But prepare yourself now, Lady,
To go with me to Brunswick,

For here is no time to linger:                            680
If your father Red Lion heard about us
He'd bring disgrace on us both
And we would be shamed for ever.

*Florentine*
O noble Duke Gloriant,
Brunswick I'd love to see!                                685
If that could happen, truly
I would go wherever you wish.

*The Duke*
O Florentine, worthy lady
Whom I love above all women,
I will make you the Duchess                               690
Of Brunswick, the good country,
I pledge my faith to that,
Noble woman of high descent.

*Florentine*
Then I'll take up the journey with you
Rather than with any other man                            695
That I ever saw with my eyes!
Noble duke, high baron,
Now let's sit here in the meadow
Until the moon has set;
Then all will be asleep                                   700
Who belong to my father's court;
Then we may go without trouble
Without meeting any one.

*The Duke*
That seems good to me, noble lady,
For I'm so overcome by sleep                              705

That I cannot stay on my feet;
I must lay my head to rest.

*Florentine*
So lay it down in my lap
And sleep, my noble hero,
And then we will leave Abelant.                                710

[*Somewhere else in Abelant*]

*Florant, Red Lion's nephew*
Help, Mohammed and Apollo!
How is the maiden Florentine
So foolishly inclined;
No man received her love,
Not even the best in heathendom;                               715
Whether high-born or handsome
She wouldn't give anyone her heart
And now she loves a Christian
And wants to leave her land for him!
Eternal shame will go to her                                   720
If I keep still about it.
By my God Tervagant,
I won't! I'll tell her father,
For I have seen it all.
Where are you, high-born baron,                                725
Red Lion, King of Abelant?
Wake up, man of high birth,
Put on your clothes in haste:
You shall hear things you don't know.

*Red Lion*
Now I'm here without delay,                                    730
Nephew Florant, what is happening?

*Florant*

Noble uncle, I have seen
Strange things about lovely Florentine,
Who rightly could be the choice
Of the Sultan of Babylon.                            735
She lies there in embrace
In yonder garden, brave hero,
With a man from Christenland,
The noble Duke of Brunswick.
I'll show you, come with me,                          740
Noble lord of wide renown,
For I have stolen his sword,
Where he lies with the noble lady.
And his horse named Valentif
I have taken from him in secret;                      745
He has come all the way from Brunswick
Where he is the Duke of the land.
Now look, man of noble birth,
Where he lies with his head in her lap.


*Red Lion*

Alas, I marvel greatly                                750
At my daughter Florentine!
There was never so noble a Saracen
That she would give her heart to him;
Now she lies here with a Christian,
Who does not belong to our faith!                     755
Alas, what has come upon her;
What shame she has brought
Onto my God Tervagant!
She shall burn in fire for that,
And the duke shall not escape                         760
From here: I'll capture him

And hang him from a tree.
By my God Apollo,
Let us go, nephew Florant
And capture the noble baron.                                765

*Florant*
Good reason we have for that, uncle,
For he is without his weapons.
Get up, high-born companion,
Brave hero of Brunswick.
You will possess Abelant,                                  770
The sweet city, the handsome jewel;
A castle is hidden in there
And you will be its keeper.
It is set on a handsome square;
You cannot find its equal.                                 775

*The Duke*
May God damn and punish you,
Angry Saracen, nasty scoundrel!
By my faith, it will cost you your life
That you did offend me today!

*Florant*
Noble lord with your honorable heart,                      780
Tone down your haughtiness;
Haughty hearts were never good
For you must remain defeated
And we shall take your life:
You have deserved your death.                              785

*The Duke*
Alas, this game is spoiled
For I have lost my sword;

May God who was born from a maiden
Destroy the man who took it
And came to me in secret                    790
While I lay here in bliss!
I have reason to lament
That I have lost my sword;
By my faith, if I had it in my hand
You'd not catch me, nasty wretch.           795

*Red Lion*
Duke, let be these angry words!
Your pride must now be cut down.
I intend for you to pay
For what your ancestors did.
Before Abelant I saw the defeat            800
Of my father by your party;
Gerald of Normandy did that;
He defeated my dear father.
And your father, by Apollo,
Beat my uncle Isembart                     805
And two knights of high descent,
My aunt's children, you should know;
They were born in the town of Antioch.
Your father killed them with his might
And you shall pay the price,               810
By my God Apollo.
As for my daughter Florentine—
I will have her killed by fire!

*The Duke*
O noble lord of Abelant,
Do with me as you please;                  815
But Florentine deserves
To be honored before any man;

For, by the father who begot me,
A chaste person is she most surely:
She was never any man's wife yet,                820
At no time, I know that well;
She is a noble creature—
So have mercy on her, noble baron.


*Red Lion*
By my God Tervagant,
I wouldn't for all the world!                    825
She will burn for what has happened:
That she ever received greetings from you.


*The Duke*
O sovereign King of Heaven,
Preserve that noble lady!
Let me lose my life if I must                    830
But preserve the lovely Florentine.
I pray you, beloved Creator,
That she may escape this death
And receive the Christian faith.
Maiden-mother, I pray you for this, too,         835
For her heart is so pure,
Entirely noble is her nature!
Mother of God, keep the lovely creature!
I beg you too, God, by your meekness,
For true love was the cause                       840
That we are in this distress.
O God, do not forget
That love also brought about
That you took on human nature
On that blessed vine                             845

That was Mary, the chaste virgin,
Who conceived you in her pure body—
It never happened to any woman—
And, virgin, she gave birth to you.
The force of love accomplished that!                    850
And later you died a bitter death
In order to bring us to bliss.
Lead me now out of this prison.


*Florentine*
Where are you, Roger, brave knight,
My dear and faithful friend?                             855


*Roger*
Here I am, noble lady,
Tell me what I can do for you.


*Florentine*
O Roger, all my refuge
Now resides altogether in you!
Dear Roger, tell me now:                                 860
What does my father say?


*Roger*
Noble lady, he has sworn,
By Mohammed and his tooth,
That he'll hang the noble hero
And deliver you to be burned;                            865
He has sworn to that so solemnly
That we had better believe it;
Therefore I am, noble lady,
Not a moment without sorrow.

*Florentine*

Noble Roger, be loyal to me,                                                    870
For to do that you have the power.
I know that you guard the dungeon
Where the duke lies detained;
Now be of assistance to him
That he may stay alive.                                                         875

*Roger*

O noble, beloved lady,
If I do that it is my death!
All the red gold in this world
Would not be of help to me.

*Florentine*

Roger, help me out of my sorrow                                                 880
And Duke Gloriant as well;
Then we will leave Abelant
For the worthy land of Brunswick.
I promise you, Roger, most certain,
I will always be your friend.                                                   885

*Roger*

Noble lady, you do deserve this,
For long before this time
Your father once swore to my death;
Then you were my only recourse.
Now I'd behave like a scoundrel                                                 890
If I forgot all that;
Though I might be quartered for it
I'll help you, noble lady,
That you may stay alive;
And also the Duke of Brunswick                                                  895

For he received me so kindly
When I brought your message to him.
I'll labor for this day and night,
Noble lady with a chaste heart;
I will unlock the dungeon                               900
And deliver the great hero.
Where are you, Sir Gloriant,
Noble duke and high baron?
Come out of this weighty prison
For all the locks are opened.                           905

*The Duke*
Who has done me this favor?
Roger, friend, inform me of that.

*Roger*
It was Florentine; she begged me
To help you out of your distress.

*The Duke*
God, who let himself be crucified,                      910
Have praise for this and thanks
That I'm out of this stinking hole
Where I have been for so long!
Now tell me: where is Florentine,
That most beautiful creature?                           915

*Roger*
Noble sir, she is locked within
Four walls and held fast;
No one can go to her
For her father wants her life.

*The Duke*
What he wants will not be done!                          920
If God preserve my life
I will free the noble lady
Before I depart from here.
If only I had my trusty steed
Valentif here at hand—                                    925
And my sword, the good weapon—
Then I would free Florentine
And settle accounts with Red Lion,
Make him pay all that he owes me!
He will regret, to be sure,                               930
That he holds her so miserably.

*Roger*
My lord, I will help you in that
And get out of the land with you.
I will bring shame to Mohammed
And take on the Christian faith.                          935
Now see here, noble knight,
Your good horse Valentif
And your good sword as well,
That your heart is longing for.

*The Duke*
Now if only I had my sweet burden,                        940
The lovely Florentine!
Dear Roger, may God reward you;
Show me now the heavy dungeon
Where the sweet maiden lies;
I'll unlock it and open the door,                         945
And if Red Lion finds out,
I will get back at him.

*Roger*
My lord, then we'd be lost,
Rousing the court and all men!
I'll find us a better way out.                                    950
You stay here in the bushes
And I will go to Red Lion
And put the idea in his head
That tomorrow he must, in haste,
Have her killed, the noble woman,                                 955
Florentine, take her life;
I will fool him with that.
You will stay here in this bush
And be steadfast on the alert.
When they bring out Florentine                                    960
In order to kill her,
Then you will come instantly
Riding up, noble baron.
By my God Tervagant,
I will be at your side;                                           965
You will stab and I will strike
And God will be our helper;
And that's the way you and I
Will free noble Florentine.


*The Duke*
It will cost me my life, dear Roger,                              970
If I don't free her from this distress.
You go now in great haste;
I will stay in the woods.
O, Father, Son, and Holy Spirit,
I pray you, preserve Florentine!                                  975

*Roger*
May Mohammed and Apollo
Mahoun and Tervagant
Grant you a good day,
Noble lord of Abelant.

*Red Lion*
Roger, give me your counsel                                    980
What to do with Gloriant?

*Roger*
Noble lord of Abelant,
I will tell you and give you counsel;
Do this tomorrow in great haste:
Take Florentine, the evil woman,                               985
And have her killed forthwith
For she deserves that fate
If you weigh the case by law:
She has insulted our Gods.
And then you take Gloriant                                     990
And hang him from a tree
For if Gerald, his uncle,
Finds out that he is in prison,
Indeed, I can assure you,
He will come with great force                                  995
And with all his might
And will do us great harm.
That's why it seems best to me
That you have both of them killed.

*Red Lion*
That is a good plan, Roger;                                    1000
I will not wait another hour!

Go and fetch me that fine lady,
Florentine, the nasty slut!
I'll have her led outside the walls
And have her head cut off!                              1005

*Roger*
My lord, that seems best to me;
I will get her, by Apollo.
Where are you, pretty Florentine?
You must go before the high lord
Your father, Red Lion.                                 1010
He will mete out justice.
He intends to make you pay
For having defiled his gods,
And also for having slept
Beside Gloriant, noble lady;                            1015
That will cost you your noble life.
He swore a dear oath to that.

*Florentine*
God, who was born from a maiden
And suckled his food from her;
And after that he suffered                              1020
The cruel Jews to take him
And hang him on the cross,
Where he died a bitter death
To bring us to great bliss:
May He have mercy on my soul.                           1025

*Red Lion*
Now tell me, daughter Florentine,
Who brought you to this point
That you are so disposed

To adore a foreign God
And mock our own gods,                                    1030
Even love a Christian man?
By my God Tervagant,
You will lose your life for this!

*Florentine*
Father, I welcome that death
For the sake of Him who died for me                       1035
And hung naked on the cross
With His arms spread wide,
His hands and His feet pierced
By three heavy nails.
Rightful God, protect me now                              1040
From the cruel fire;
And preserve Duke Gloriant
For he is in great distress!
O noble, high-born companion,
I would have loved to see you                             1045
Once more, but it cannot be;
That gives my heart great pain.

*The Hangman*
You will never see him again,
Noble and high-born lady!
I'll take your life away                                  1050
Although it breaks my heart.
O noble maiden Florentine,
How did you come to this?
If you still worshiped our Mohammed
You would still be alive.                                 1055
It's all because of your sin:
You blaspheme against our gods,

Bring shame upon yourself,
And you so nobly born!

*Red Lion*
Too long you give her respite!                              1060
Make haste, cut off her head!
For her misdeed is so great
All the world cannot help her.

*The Duke*
By God, who was crucified,
It shall not be, cruel tyrant!                              1065
May God bring shame upon you,
You are so base and vile!
Get away at this evil time
Or the devil will take care of you!
Florentine's life will be saved                            1070
And she will be mine to your shame.
O most beloved Florentine,
You are saved now from this death,
Thanks be to Mary the noble virgin
And to that brave hero Roger.                               1075

*Florentine*
O noble Duke Gloriant,
I thank God in heaven for this—
That all turned out so well for me!
And I thank also you and Roger,
Valiant lord; let us get away                               1080
From here, lord of noble birth.

*The Duke*
Florentine, let us now

Go to my land of Brunswick.
My heart overflows with joy,
Noble woman of high descent.                                    1085

*[They approach Brunswick]*

Now I see the precious garden,
Brunswick, the good country.
Noble uncle, valiant knight,
High baron of Normandy,
Have the gate thrown wide open                                  1090
And joyfully let her enter
Whom I love with all my heart:
Lovely Florentine of Abelant!

*Gerald*
Gloriant my nephew,
Welcome to you on this day!                                     1095
Welcome, Florentine, I never
Saw you before this day;
My heart opens wide in joy
That I see you with the lady
Returning alive and sound.                                      1100
How were things in Abelant?

*The Duke*
Noble uncle, valiant knight,
While asleep I was imprisoned
And thrown into a dungeon;
And I pined to get out of there                                 1105
For vipers, toads and snakes
Were my nearest neighbors there.
But God granted me good fortune:

A helping friend and good counsel
So that I could escape                                          1110
Without harm from that dark prison;
No man ever was in such fear!
But my love for the noble lady
Kept me alive all the time,
For I hoped it would turn for the better;                       1115
And so, with my persistence
I won my heart's desire.

*Gerald*
Nephew Gloriant, you have learned
To till the garden of love.
No need for you to regret,                                      1120
Though it may have been bitter at times.
You bring here a lovely creature;
She couldn't be any nobler;
Though her father is a Saracen,
He is a man of high birth:                                      1125
The Sultan of Babylon
Was his father, I know that well;
And his mother was the daughter
Of the Lord of Antioch.
Her father was praised all around                               1130
At all times in Christendom.
No one bearing arms among pagans
Is equal to him in valor.
That's why I feared for you,
That you'd come to a bad end,                                   1135
But you have done very well;
You won through perseverance.
It wouldn't do to start
Without the will to persist.

Now, peace! and let's be still.                                    1140
This first play is over—
Now we will play you a farce.

*Nota xic.xli verses*

# BLOW-IN-THE-BOX

## The Characters

The first man
The other man
The first man's wife
Gert, the neighbor

# BLOW-IN-THE-BOX

## HERE BEGINS THE FARCE

*The First Man*[6]
See now, here I am!
I'm a miller and like to drink beer;
Bags and gloves I can sew,
Hay and grain I can mow;
Yea, if I extend myself                                        5
I could also buy and sell;
Or be a carpenter as well—
Though I made no money there.
I'm a miller and I can grind,
I can borrow and not pay back;                                10
Cut down trees and chop them up;
I can brew and I can bake,
I can build dikes and dams,
I can thresh and also winnow,
And lots of other things as well.                            15
Is there any lady or gent
Who will hire me as a servant?
'Tis true, I like to sleep late
And drag my feet at work.
Would any one check me out                                    20
And hire me for a servant's job?
For I can linger at the table
As well as I dig and pick flax.

---

[6]Duinhoven (1994) argues that the opening speech is more likely to be spoken by the bragging charlatan and posits that the captions in the beginning have been mixed up. *The Other Man* would then be the older man being hoodwinked. This thesis is attractive but it requires extensive textual manipulation. The older man would not speak until line 42.

*The Other Man*
And I can repair stoneware crocks
And milk basins of earthenware.                                    25

*First Man*
A devil of a wind blows you here
With your bag of crazy tricks!

*The Other Man*
God give you cramp in your jaws
If you think these are tricks!
I'd as lief earn my bread just like you                            30
With a wife and children at home!

*First Man*
Well, it seems funny business to me
To fix earthen crocks and bowls!
If you can really make them whole
You must be a mighty clever man.                                   35

*The Other Man*
You think I can't do more than that?
If I really exert myself
And open up my bag of tricks
I could turn you into a horse!
'Twould seem well worth ten pounds!                                40
A black one with a shaggy mane.

*First Man*
God has brought me to you;
I can hear you're a real genius!
Could you rid me of my grey hairs

And make me look ten years younger                     45
So that I would please my wife?
I would pay you handsomely.


*The Other Man*
Sure, I'll make you look so good
Your wife will be raving about you!
If I let you blow in this box                          50
You'll take on a different hue;
You'll be spiffed up in such a way
Your wife would not know you again.

*First Man*
By my faith, you will gain big
If that could happen to me!                            55

*The Other Man*
By God, your wife will notice
When you get back to her!

*The First Man*
Then I wouldn't be damned any more,
Though it cost me my last mite!
She always yells I'm ugly                               60
And I rarely live in peace.
Here, see what I will give you:
This good purse and the money too!
I sold my good cow yesterday;
This is all the money I've got.                         65
It will be yours altogether:
Ten shillings and forty pounds.

*The Other Man*
Here, put this box at your mouth
And blow hard, with all your strength.
*[Aside]* I've pulled off so may feats,                    70
I'll manage this one withal.


*First Man*
Will my voice be better as well?
I never could learn to sing.


*The Other Man*
Oh sure, your color will change
And your voice will be all clear.                    75


*First Man*
Jeez, God give you a good year!
I'll be grateful, no matter the price;
If I also learn to sing
The money will be well-spent.


*The Other Man*
Now blow and may God bless you.                    80
Now boy, what a man are you now!
I swear to you by Saint John,
There's no man alive today,
Who never saw you before
And who would not know you now.[7]                    85

---

[7]Probably a deliberately scrambled statement, whereby the trickster avoids a clear lie and also, indirectly, demonstrates his victim's obtuseness. The Dutch has: *Ic swere u bi sente jan/Dat hi niet en leeft op desen dach/Die u met oghen noit en sach/Dat hi u niet kinnen en sal.*

*First Man*
Now God willing and with luck,
How shall I make out with my wife?
Only four or five days ago
She called me an ugly thing;
Now I'll go home right away                              90
And see how she likes me now!
She has made so many complaints
That I was ugly and old.
Now I can't be blamed any more:
I have a new skin on my face!                            95


*The Other Man [Aside]*
Well done, and the money is in the bag!


*First Man*
Faith, I can jump much better now!
With God's help I'll sing a clear song:
"Thanks and praise be to God!"
My singing has also improved,                           100
As much as my handsome face.
O sweet little wife let me in
And come have a look at me!


*His Wife*
Jeez, look at this scarecrow here!
What devil made you such a fright?                       105


*The First Man* (her Husband)
I have bathed in the fountain of youth!
Don't you like the look of me now?
This handsome face has cost
The whole price of our cow.

*His Wife*
Faith, the devil has my thanks!                                                       110
Did you give your money for this?

*The First Man*
Right, and nothing is left of it now;
With the money, I gave him the purse.
And he held a little box to my mouth;
I blew in it with all my strength                                                     115
And so much power came out
That now I'm as handsome as this!

*His Wife*
Jeez, hear this and praise the Lord!
A wife will do well with this man!
Faith, the devil gave him to me;                                                      120
You are black as a blackamoor.

*The First Man*
What the devil, do I look such a fright?
And don't I look nice, white and bright?

*His Wife*
You're a good-for-nothing, for sure;
I never saw an uglier creature.                                                       125
Hey Gert, dear neighbor, come see,
Take a look here at my man.

*Gert* (his neighbor)
Why Gosen, by Saint John,
Who made you look such a fright?
You look like you washed in a dye vat—                                                130
Your face is all covered in black.

*The First Man*
Aye me, am I all disgusting?
Is it really truly so?
Let me look in a clear mirror
So I can see for myself.                                    135

*His Wife*
For sure, you shall have it.

*The First Man*
Help, help, you good people!
I never saw a thing like this.
No man was ever so cheated!

*His Wife*
And you thought that I was lying,              140
You filthy old ass!

*The First Man*
That's the truth, so help me God,
I can really be called a fool.
O my sweetest, sweetest love,
Help me to get this off.                                   145

*His Wife*
By God, I don't care a straw
If you looked like this forever.

*The First Man*
I can tell you don't care at all
If I am transformed like this.
Good neighbor, dear Gert,                           150
How can I get rid of this?

*Gert*
We'll have to scour you with piss
And with other things like that.

*The First Man*
Help, help! I will be smothered
If you treat me with old piss!                                    155

*His Wife*
I wish I had the money for the cow
That you spent so well on this!
And I wish you'd bathe in a cesspool,
You dirty old wretch!

*The First Man*
No matter how nasty you are,                                      160
And whatever you have to say,
I'd spend the price of our sow
To get rid of this stuff.

*His Wife*
Jeez, look at this here man
And the looks that he just bought!                                165

*The First Man*
The villain made me believe
That I'd be handsome and sing well,
I'd be young and skip and jump,
And that I would please you no end.

*Gert*
You have to hand it to him,                                       170
By God: he did mean well.

*His Wife*
Jeez, neighbor, don't talk about it!
You get me all upset.
He deserves that I beat him silly
And don't let him into the house.                    175

*The First Man*
In name of Christ and the devil,
I didn't complain this loud
When you wasted all the money
From the other cow on that Brother
And lent him my good grey gown                        180
That he pawned for bed and board!
It's a shame to say it, I know,
But I'm telling the neighbors about it.

*Gert*
Jeez, neighbor, shut your mouth!
You'd bring shame on your wife.                       185

*His Wife*
God give him cramp in his jaws!
How can you say that of me?

*The First Man*
The jerk was right on top of you,
And his bird was on your seat!
Right alongside he lay, not across—                  190
I saw very well what you did!
I was never content again,
Since I saw you with your bare knees.

*His Wife*
I might have been looking for fleas,
You filthy old man!                                    195

*The First Man*
What the devil did the Brother do,
Rolling and thrashing about?

*His Wife*
God give you the cramp, dirty wretch,
We were just playing games.

*The First Man*
Well, I do not like those games;                       200
I do not like them at all!

*His Wife*
Shut up, it's a shame you're alive,
You filthy beast, you!
I'll hit you in your teeth.


*Nota iic.vi verses*


*[Epilogue]*

Good people the play is over;                          205
You may go home now.
Go down the steps, all of you—
If you liked it, be sure to come back.

# LANCELOT OF DENMARK

## The Characters

Lancelot of Denmark
His Mother
Sandrine, a maiden who serves Lancelot's mother
Reynold, Lancelot's Chamberlain
A Knight
The Knight's Forest Keeper

# AN *ABEL* PLAY OF LANCELOT OF DENMARK

# HOW HE FELL IN LOVE, WITH A MAIDEN

# WHO SERVED HIS MOTHER

## AND A FARCE TO FOLLOW

### [Prologue]

I pray to God on his throne
And to Mary the lovely maiden
That they preserve us all
And keep us virtuous as well,
So that we may gain his kingdom.                                    5
For this I pray Mary the queen,
Who is our supreme lady.
Now hear what we will play for you!
It's about an excellent knight
In love with a noble lady,                                          10
Courteous and chaste of heart,
But she was too low for him
In wealth and also of birth.
Therefore his mother was vexed
That he loved so far beneath him.                                   15
His heart always glowed with joy
When he saw the noble lady,
But his mother, that nasty woman,
Was always chagrined and angry
And often she reproached him                                        20
That he would demean himself,
But he always defended himself

With the most courteous words he could
And always he kept his affection
For the lovely lady Sandrine.                                25
She couldn't have a nobler character
(But was too lowly born for him)
So his mother remained chagrined
And she acted on that, later on.
Now I pray you that you will                                 30
Pay attention and consider;
I bet you never heard of love
As you will hear of it now!
Now I pray you, rich and poor,
That you will stop talking                                   35
And note how we will start.

*Lancelot*
Oh God, how can it be
That I have lost my heart
To the lovely Sandrine,
But every day I hear                                         40
Reproaches from my mother
That I lower myself in love,
And I hear many sneering words;
But love for her has pierced me
And I cannot stop loving now.                                45
Always I want to speak,
When I see her with my eyes.
For this my mother is pained
And I have to hide my love.
Now I will wait for my lady                                  50
Under this sweetbrier;
She will be here shortly
In this garden, I am sure.

*Sandrine*
O noble knight of high descent,
May God, the All-powerful,     55
Grant you a good day,
Noble knight with courteous heart.

*Lancelot*
Lovely maiden, may God be with us
And keep us both in good virtue
And preserve us from evil,     60
From the jealous talk of spies,
So that they will not proclaim
Evil stories about us two!
O Sandrine, now advise me:
My heart is all stirred up     65
And tormented with love for you,
So that it will cost me my life,
O Sandrine, lovely lady.
If I cannot have you as my own,
It will cost me my life     70
And I will be lost forever!

*Sandrine*
Noble knight of high descent,
That should never happen.
I am very fond of you,
But I am not your equal;     75
You are too mighty and wealthy
For me to be your wife,
So that is the end of that.
Though I love you with all my heart,
I will not be any man's lover,     80
Whoever he may be;

He might be a king with a crown,
I would not throw myself away.

*Lancelot*
Lovely maiden with your pure heart,
If you let me have my will,                                    85
Most beloved Sandrine,
It would not go unrewarded.
Unexpected things might happen!
You might still be my wife.
Have mercy on me and trust me                                 90
And come with me to this castle
And I will give you a jewel,
Unlike anything you've seen.

*Sandrine*
Noble sir, I am yet a virgin;
For that I thank God in heaven.                               95
Even if you would reward me
With a thousand marks in gold,
High baron and noble companion,
I would rather keep forever
My chastity. I may not be wealthy                            100
And my ancestors may not be noble,
But I mean to protect myself,
So people will not brand me
Any man's mistress,
But gladly I will share true love                            105
With you, without any scandal.

*Lancelot*
Sandrine, by the Virgin Mary,
I do not wish anything common!

No woman is born on this earth
So wealthy, mighty and lovely,                           110
That she'd make me more happy than you!
Oh Sandrine, will you then
Leave me in this sorrow?
Will you not have pity on me
And will I have no solace?                               115
Let us dally in the woods
Or down in this green valley,
Where the birds are all singing
And the flowers bloom in the grass,
Dear maiden, without misdeeds                            120
And without any villainy!

*Sandrine*
Sir Lancelot, it's often said:
Easy trust leads to easy deception.
That is certainly true and no lie.
It has often happened                                   125
That women have been dishonored
Because they trusted too lightly!
And later they much regretted
Whatever happened to them.
I would not know on this earth                           130
Any man I would trust so far,
And who wouldn't force his way
If I'd dally with him in the woods.

*Lancelot*
I love you too much for that,
Lovely lady Sandrine,                                   135
I wouldn't dishonor you
Even if I could, lovely maiden;

I never had it in mind
To bring shame upon you.
If I had you in a far country,                          140
Most beloved Sandrine,
I'd sooner go begging for you
Than allow you to go hungry!
By my knighthood I wouldn't do
Anything against your will!                             145

*Sandrine*

Sir Lancelot, we've been here too long.
Someone might see or hear us.
Jealous people are always spying
To bring scandal upon others;
A traitor would rather tell                             150
Bad tales than good. It's his nature.
Let us quickly part from each other
That no one may take offense,
High-born knight, noble prince,
May the lord God preserve you                           155
And keep you virtuous always,
Wherever you may go.

*Lancelot*

My heart remains in sorrow
For the lovely Sandrine!
She'll not let me have my way                           160
And I will mourn forever.
However I wail and complain,
She won't go with me into the woods.
She would rather have honor than gold;
I can tell that from her manner.                        165

She leads a chaste life
And her heart is so noble!
By my knighthood, I would wish
That she were born my equal;
Though she might not be wealthy,                    170
I would make her my wife.
For she is a chaste lady
And her heart is full of honor,
But she will not turn towards me
And my heart suffers great mourning.                175

*His Mother*
Lancelot of Denmark,
I have heard your courting.
By the Virgin Mary, Lancelot,
I can't help being astonished
That you don't hold yourself higher                180
And that you love so far beneath you!
You stand here so weakly and cry
For one who cares little for you.
Fie, 'tis a shame that you live
And love such a common woman!                       185

*Lancelot*
O mother, she is so chaste;
Her heart is so vivacious
And her person is so gracious,
I have to love her always!
My heart is all aglow                               190
When I see her with my eyes.
Dear mother, noble lady,
I love her whatever happens.

*His Mother*
Take a look at yourself, my son:
You are handsome and nobly born!                    195
You should act as I advise you
And love one who is your equal.

*Lancelot*
In all Christendom I don't know
Whom I'd rather have than Sandrine!
I wish she could be mine!                           200
Dear mother, grant me this:
Even if I owned the whole world,
'Tis her I would want as my wife.

*His Mother*
You wretch, be ashamed of yourself,
That you love so far below you!                     205
You can find just as lovely ladies
Of noble families born.

*Lancelot*
Dear mother, the force of love
Won't regard birth or wealth.
It looks for a mate of the soul,                    210
For the two to be equal in essence.
I have often heard it told
That love seeks its own kind;
Though one lover may be poor and one rich,
Noble love will bring it about.                     215
True love pays no attention
To riches or noble birth;
Never did so at any time!
It all happens by Fortune;

Let noble love have its way;                                   220
It cares not for high birth.

*His Mother*
O Lancelot, how your heart
Is overcome by Sandrine!
If you will do as I want
I'll see that you have your will                               225
Tonight, in all secrecy,
In your room, worthy knight,
And do with her as you wish,
If you promise me one thing.

*Lancelot*
By Saint Simeon, Lady mother,                                  230
I'll promise whatever you want
If I can have and enjoy her
In my room, just she and I!

*His Mother*
Just promise me, Lancelot,
By your knighthood and your faith,                             235
When you have had your way
With the maiden Sandrine,
You will say "I've had enough;
Now I'm overfull of you
And so gorged in my heart                                      240
As from eating seven sides of bacon."
Be sure that you do not forget
To say these words to her
And then you will, right away,
Turn your back for the whole night                             245

And sleep fine and well
And not speak a single word.

*Lancelot*
Mother dear, is that what you want?
That I speak such low, common words?
I never heard such a thing!                        250
What good might that do you
That I would speak like that
To Sandrine from my own mouth
And lie there like a dog,
Without speaking, like a wretch!                   255
What would the chaste lady think?
That I would behave so low,
While I have such love for her?
It would hurt me in my heart.

*His Mother*
Lancelot, that is what I want.                      260
If you want her in your power,
You must promise me that, like a man,
And carry it out with honor.

*Lancelot*
Lady mother, bring her then;
I'll do whatever you wish                           265
Though it pains me in my heart.
But people often say things
That they don't mean, as I will do.
Although my mouth will say it,
I will not mean it deep down,                       270
For I only wish her well.
I pray to God in Heaven

That she will not blame me for it!
She is so noble and good,
If she would take offense                               275
Her heart might turn from me
And my heart would remain in pain.

*His Mother [to the audience]*
That's exactly what I want:
To separate you two.
Don't you see how he would behave!                      280
He's the highest in the land
And brings such shame upon himself
As to love such a lowborn woman!
He'd marry her, the wretch,
I can tell, if I would let him.                         285
I'll arrange it otherwise
So that it will never happen.
Where are you lovely Sandrine?
Come here, I must speak to you.

*Sandrine*
Noble lady, here I am.                                  290
Please tell me what you desire.

*His Mother*
Sandrine, my heart is oppressed
And I must confide my worry to you:
Here is my dear son, Lancelot,
By sickness so overcome,                                295
So badly struck last night,
That he has not spoken since.
I don't know what may ail him
Or what may be causing him pain,

But when this morning came,                                         300
He gave such a deep sigh!
Sandrine, I fear for his life.
My heart suffers for him.
I beg you, lovely Sandrine,
Please go to Lancelot,                                              305
For he is gravely afflicted;
This weighs me down with sorrow.


*Sandrine*
Noble lady, what you command
I will be glad to do;
I'll be happy to go with you,                                       310
For I don't want him to suffer.


*His Mother [Aside]*
Look out for yourself at the right time
And you will hold your own.
This is the way to contrive
To get the woman in the trap.                                       315
Who'd do that better than I?
For when he's had his way
His love will pass away.
It's happened many times.


*Now she has been with him in his room* [8]
*[During the following speech, Sandrine moves from Denmark to the forest]*


*Sandrine*
Oh God who was crucified,                                           320

_____

[8]It is not clear whether this is a line of the mother's dialogue or intended as a kind
of stage direction. The text fails to indicate that Sandrine speaks the next lines.

How false is Lancelot's mother!
I know that better now
Than I did last night.
She told me a blatant lie,
That he was down and sick;                                    325
She led me into the trap
And told me lies for truth,
And brought me into Lancelot's power.
I will regret this forever!
But more than that I resent                                   330
The words that the noble knight spoke,
When he turned away from me
As if I were a stinking dog.
That is stuck fast deep inside me
And hurts my heart so much!                                   335
I'll take care that he will never more
Hear good or bad about me.
I'm leaving to go my way,
Wandering in strange lands.
I pray God that he will hide                                  340
The shame that I have received,
For I did it against my will;
Now I am sad at heart.
Lancelot, you will nevermore see me!
I'll wander in this forest.                                   345
O Father, Son, Holy Spirit,
I pray you preserve me now,
So that I don't have to be
Some man's wife, in shame,
In whatever land I may be;                                    350
That I may remain as I am!
I pray for this, Mother and Maiden,
Wellspring of all purity,

That no man may propose
Coarse and villainous deeds.                                   355
I pray for this, wellspring of virtues,
Worthy Mother and Maiden.
There I see a lovely spring;
On that spot I will take a rest.
I have fasted for so long                                      360
That I'm hungry and thirsty too;
I have such a desire to drink
That I can't bear it any longer.


*The Knight*
God willing I shall go hunting;
I pray to God in heaven                                        365
And to the maiden Mary
That they preserve me now
And give me favor and luck
To hunt and catch some prey.
I haven't caught a thing for so long                           370
And I'm ashamed with good reason;
For four days I have hunted,
But not even a rabbit have I found!
I am ashamed in my heart
That my effort is so useless.                                  375
Now I will sound my horn
And see if God will provide.


                    *Now he sounds his horn*
By the Lord who created me,
I see some game there stirring
That my heart is eager for!                                    380
I don't think any man saw
Such handsome game any day
As yonder at that stream;

A lovely innocent maiden
She seems to be by her looks.                            385
O God, how may I catch her?
Then my efforts wouldn't be lost.
I will sound my horn again
And see how she behaves.


*He sounds the horn again*
O God, who is Lord above all,                           390
Grant me now the chance
That I may have my way
With this lovely creature.
Lovely maiden, please stand still!
My prisoner you must be,                                395
More desirable than a wild boar,
Even one made all of gold.
I thank God for this lovely catch,
And for getting up early this morning.


*Sandrine*
Excellent noble knight,                                 400
Do not do anything base!
By your rank I pray you that
You do not do anything vile.
It would be a reproach to you,
If you came to any court.                               405
You look like a praiseworthy knight;
Therefore I pray you, dear baron,
That you do not treat me ill
But leave me as I am.


*The Knight*
Lovely lady, please tell me:                            410
From where did you come to this forest?

My mind marvels at this,
That I find you thus alone
In this forest, at this stream.
What is it that holds you here? 415
Has someone promised to meet you,
Someone that you're waiting for?
He might be a man of power;
I'd not like to speak to you then.

*Sandrine*
Noble knight, 'tis not for a man 420
That I stand here, high-born baron;
Other things have brought me here.
I have wandered from the place
Where I lived in joy and honor.
I wandered, I don't know where, 425
And stand here in great fear
And don't know where to go.
To God I bewail my misfortune
That I must endure this world.

*The Knight*
Now I thank God for my good fortune, 430
That I got up early this morning
And encountered such noble beauty,
Found her while I'm hunting!
God has brought us together,
I know that most certainly. 435
You were born just for me,
For you please me very much:
Your looks and your courteous words,
All these give me great pleasure.
We will be joyful together. 440

Now come with me to my castle;
You never saw such a beauty!
It will be yours and mine.

*Sandrine*
Sir knight, let be these words;
I pray you by God Almighty                                          445
That you don't trifle with me,
Even though I may be lost.

*The Knight*
Lovely lady, my heart is now
Altogether inflamed by love.
You are courteous and comely;                                      450
By my knighthood, you'll be my wife!
You are such a lovely person;
If you're willing and so inclined,
I pray you, tell me your name;
You will certainly be my lady.                                     455

*Sandrine*
Noble knight, if this is the truth,
I will tell you my name:
I am called Sandrine
And my father's name was Robert;
He was a well-born squire                                          460
And served the king of Auvergne.[9]

---

[9]The manuscript has *Averne*, which is usually read as "Auvergne," although that
area in France was never a kingdom. Recently, it has been suggested that it actually
refers to Navarre (See Van Anrooij and Sleiderink, 1994). For a different view, see
Kuiper (1997).

*The Knight*

Lovely lady, I'm glad to hear it,
That you are of noble descent.
Now I thank God for the good fortune
That I didn't sleep late this morning.                    465
'T was an angel that called me,
To go hunt in the forest!
My eyes never saw sweeter woman.
You will certainly be mine.

*Sandrine*

Sir knight, if it will be thus,                           470
I'll gladly turn to you
And thank God and you for the honor
In your condescending to me.
You have talked to me so kindly,
With courteous and handsome words.                        475
I pray God that he reward you
For being so courteous at heart,
And for having at this time
Spoken so kindly to me.

*The Knight*

Lovely maiden, let us go then;                            480
I pledge you my faith.

*Sandrine*

Let us go then into this park,
Sir knight, to talk a bit,
And mark well my words.
I beg you this, noble baron:                              485
Look at this handsome green tree,

How full of blossoms it stands.
The perfume of it spreads around
Throughout this whole orchard.
In such a sweet valley it stands                                   490
That it just has to bloom.
It is so noble and sweet,
It's an ornament to this orchard.
If a noble falcon came,
Flying down onto this tree,                                         495
To pick a flower from it
And never another thereafter,
And never more than that one,
Would you hate the tree for that reason
And refuse to take it therefore?                                   500
I pray you: answer me that,
And tell me the full truth,
Noble knight, in courteous words.

*The Knight*
Lovely lady, I understand you:
One blossom is as nothing;                                         505
If nothing more happened
I would not hate the tree for that reason,
Or refuse to take it therefore,
For it is formed in beauty
And I see many blossoms on it,                                      510
Far more than can be counted.
Noble fruit will come from that tree,
If God will grant it so.
No further word about this
And come with me, dear woman.                                      515

[*Back in Denmark*]

*Lancelot*

Alas, I have lost all joy
That I ever had in this world
Because I can find her nowhere,
The most lovely Sandrine.
Cursed be my mother                                        520
That I ever spoke those words!
I thought my heart would break,
When I spoke those cruel words.
That's why she is angry with me
And has secretly gone from here.                           525
It's all my mother's fault;
She made me speak those words.
I will nevermore be content
Until I see that noble woman.
O, I love her innocent person                              530
So much that I feel myself languish.
Being with her would be life,
For she is ever so noble.
She is an eminent lady,
Empress of my five senses.                                 535
No man could love a woman
As much as I love her, or more.
I'll have a search for her everywhere
That she might be in Christendom.
Where are you Reynold, come to me,                         540
My dearest chamberlain.


*Reynold*

Noble lord, what is the reason
That you stand here in lamentation?

*Lancelot*
Alas, I was never so wretched
As I am at this hour,                                         545
Because I have thus lost
The lovely creature Sandrine!
I think my heart will break
From the great grief that I suffer.
That I don't take leave of my senses                         550
Is really a great marvel.
I would much rather be dead
Than never see her again.
Reynold, you must go search
If you can find her somewhere,                               555
For I'll nevermore be joyful
Till I see her with my eyes.
Reynold, be faithful to me;
Go look for her East and South
And tell her I'll make her my bride,                         560
My family notwithstanding.

*Reynold*
I gladly venture my life
For that, and spare no effort,
But it's better for you to give up;
Who knows how she'll respond?                                565

*Lancelot*
O she is so full of honor
And so innocent in person,
I know she wouldn't lower herself
For all the goods on this earth;
I know that for the truth.                                   570
She is noble in her thoughts!

Hasten Reynold, as much as you can.
Go look for her East and North
And South and West, on and on,
Until you have found her;                                              575
For my heart does faithfully love her
And I never saw anyone sweeter.


*[In the forest]*


*The Knight's Forest Keeper*
With good reason I complain:
So many years have I
Wandered here and there,                                              580
As a forester for my lord
And guarded over his forest,
The wellspring in this woodland,
And often walked on the banks,
Many days and many hours,                                             585
But never once I chanced
To observe a woman here.
Of this I complain with reason!
Never did one cross my path,
But yesterday my lord got up[10]                                      590
To go hunting in the forest—
I don't think I ever saw a woman
As lovely as the one he found!
He took her hand very kindly
And happily brought her to court.                                     595
If she were an empress
She couldn't be more noble!

---

[10]In line 654 the Forest Keeper says that it was "now almost a year ago," which seems more likely.

Sandrine is her name;
He made her his wedded wife.
Good reason have I to grieve,                               600
For it never happened to me.
By God, I will keep my eyes open
At all times, early and late;
If I caught such a sweet red mouth
I would be the happier for it,                              605
And I would with all my heart
Thank God for the rest of my days.
Now I will hide in these bushes
And wait to see what happens.

*[During the following speech, Reynold moves from*
*Denmark to the forest]*

*Reynold*
O Mary, mother and maiden,                                 610
I pray to you for your guidance
To get a good clear answer
About Sandrine's whereabouts.
My lord, Sir Lancelot,
Is so dismayed in his heart                                615
And tormented with love for her
That he cannot endure it;
The only regret of his heart
Is that he has lost her like this.
Now he has sworn by his knighthood                         620
To marry her, if I can find her,
For he is so full of sorrow
That he has lost her like this
That he lives in great suffering,
And all from true love!                                    625

Oh God, if I could find her,
I would be joyful and happy.
Deus God, who can tell me
What that man there has in mind?
His face seems to be so angry                           630
And his club is heavy and big.
He must be a murderer,
Unless my fear deceives me.
I'll ride to him nonetheless
For I think he is by himself.                            635
I never saw a man by himself
That I was fearful of.
Friend, God give you a good day
And a favorable morning,
And may God grant you to be                              640
Healthy at all times.

*The Knight's Forest Keeper*
God reward you, whoever you are,
For your friendly words to me.

*Reynold*
Now be so kind as to tell me:
Have you, long ago,                                      645
Seen a maiden passing
Who was lovely and graceful?

*The Knight's Forest Keeper*
Friend, you must understand me:
I have walked here many a day
And never seen any woman,                                650
Young or old, that's the truth.
But now almost a year ago

A knight, my good lord,
Got up in the morning and went
Hunting near this stream                           655
And there he found one hiding,
An innocent young maiden;
With happy heart he brought her along
And said it was a good hunt,
For he had caught a maiden,                        660
Beautiful and nobly born.

*Reynold*
Friend, I want to hear more of this:
What was her name, I beg you?

*The Knight's Forest Keeper*
Friend, you shall know the truth:
Sandrine is her name;                              665
She could not be more noble
Nor better shaped in her figure.
She is like no other woman
Living here in the land;
She's comely and good as well.                     670
He has made her his wife,
And she is so loyal to him,
Obedient and docile,
All the people around my lord
Love her for her great virtue                      675
And they all rejoice
That she belongs to the court.

*Reynold*
Now may God be my counsel,
That is the maiden I mean!

I have sought the chaste lady                              680
Many miles through many lands,
But I never came upon
Such good news as you report.
Now dear friend, do tell me:
How can I speak to her?                                    685

*The Knight's Forest Keeper*
Friend, you would never manage
To speak to my lady,
Unless it were with my help.
I am in good standing with her
And the head of all the servants                           690
That are in my lord's service.
If you would by any chance
Put a penny for a drink in my hand
You can speak to her, brave man,
As much as your heart desires.                             695

*Reynold*
A penny is easily spent
And doesn't yield much to drink!
Run and hurry as fast as you can
And let me speak with Sandrine—
Here are two red-gold coins—                               700
And tell her in forceful words:
Here's a messenger from Denmark,
In a hurry to speak to her.

*The Knight's Forest Keeper*
I will run in great haste
And bring the lady with me.                                705
O noble-hearted lady,

I beg you kindly to come.
Here outside is a proud hero
In a hurry to speak to you.

*Reynold*
Noble lady, loyal and good,                          710
May the Almighty God
Grant you a good day,
Lovely maiden Sandrine.

*Sandrine*
Welcome to you, Reynold!
Now tell me what you desire.                          715

*Reynold*
I'll tell you, worthy lady:
I want you to come with me,
For the noble knight Lancelot
Sent a search for you everywhere;
And the last command that he gave                      720
Was that, if I found you,
I should bring you to him, lady.
He will certainly make you his bride.

*Sandrine*
Reynold, that game is up!
Tell him to start another.                            725
I don't care for Lancelot's love
As much as a blade of grass.

*Reynold*
You should see his condition, Lady,
And his sad and sorry state!

From the moment that he lost you,                              730
Noble lady, he has suffered
Every single day
And lived in great torment.
It will be the death of him
If he cannot win you over,                                     735
For I know that he loves you
Above all women alive.
He swore by his knighthood
That, when he has news about you
(Though his relatives may object)                              740
You will become his wife.

*Sandrine*
Reynold, that's out of the question!
I am wedded in good faith
And have married a noble man,
Whom I love above all men,                                     745
And I do not want to forsake him.
Even if Lancelot were so mighty
To be equal to Hector of Troy;
If he had, by God's grace,
The very selfsame crown                                        750
That belonged to King Alexander,
He would still not be to my taste.
My own husband I prefer;
He bears me all his affections;
I'll always be faithful to him.                                755

*Reynold*
O lovely lady Sandrine,
If he cannot win you, then
He must live in sorrow

And in heartache forever!
This marriage that you made,                              760
You may well rue it forever
Because noble Lancelot
Would certainly have married you.

*Sandrine*
I do not regret this marriage,
Nor will I ever regret it.                                765
For I never saw a man on this earth
For whom I had more affection
Than for my dear husband—
With reason, for he deserves it.
He is a knight of wide renown,                            770
A valiant, courageous man,
Well-born and wealthy in goods,
Intelligent and wise.
He bears his arms boldly
And is known for his great deeds.                         775
My heart loves him faithfully
Above all other creatures.
Now I will no longer tarry;
Reynold, go in haste
And tell your lord Lancelot                               780
That he think of me nevermore.

*Reynold*
O noble-hearted lady,
Since it has to be like this,
I pray you, gentle lady,
For a token, so I may                                     785
Truthfully show that I saw you
And spoke to you as well.

*Sandrine*

Reynold, I will do as you ask;
I will give you, in fact,
A proper and noble token.                              790
You will tell the high-born knight
That we stood—he and I—
In a lovely green garden
And that a noble falcon,
A gentle, precious bird                                795
Perched down on a branch,
Beautiful with many flowers.
You will tell the good knight
That the falcon that came
Took from the branch one flower                        800
And left all the others standing.
Then he beat his wings
And flew away in great haste.
You will say that to the prince.
And shortly the falcon came back                       805
And searched for the branch up and down
But he could not find it again.
Then the falcon had great sorrow
That he couldn't find the branch.
You'll tell that to the brave knight.                  810
He will believe from these words
That you spoke to me in person,
If you put this story to him.
These are my final words,
Reynold, may God keep you!                             815

*Reynold*

*[During this speech, Reynold goes to Denmark]*

Alas God, now I must go
And leave the lovely lady.
I am faced with a great dilemma:
How I shall present my message?
If I tell the whole truth,                                    820
That she is alive and married,
I know we'll all regret it.
He'll want the lovely lady;
I know it'll cost him his life
And all those who are his relations              825
To the tenth degree—
He will endanger them all
And many will suffer for that
A bitter death, I am sure.
And the labor would all be in vain              830
For he could never win her;
He'd bring great trouble to himself
And also to other great men.
I will change my story somewhat
And tell him she has died.                          835
Where are you noble companion,
Bold knight of Denmark?

*Lancelot*

Welcome, dear friend Reynold,
I welcome you most warmly.
Have you heard about Sandrine                  840
Anything at all? Do tell me.

*Reynold*

Alas, noble, courtly lord,
I sought her in many countries
Until at last I found her
In a town that is called Rawast,                    845
Where the noble lady had traveled;
It's a town in Africa.
Lancelot, noble hero,
There I found the lovely lady
And that cost her her life,                          850
When she heard me speak of you;
Her noble heart did break,
When she heard me mention your name.

*Lancelot*

Reynold, those are all fables!
I can hear that you're lying to me.                  855
I don't want you to deceive me,
But tell me the whole truth.
If you brought me a token from her
Then I would sooner believe you.

*Reynold*

Lancelot, high-born man,                             860
I will give you, in fact,
A proper and noble token
That the spotless lady gave me:
She said that the two of you
Stood in a lovely green garden                       865
And that a noble falcon
A gentle, precious bird,
Perched down on a branch
Beautiful with many flowers

(She told me to say this to you)                                    870
And that the falcon that came
Took from the branch one flower
And left all the others standing;
Then he beat his wings
And flew away in great haste—                                       875
She said that to me, prince—
And shortly the falcon came back
And searched for the branch up and down
But he could not find it again.
Then the falcon had great sorrow                                    880
That he couldn't find the branch.
That is the token, brave hero,
That the noble lady gave me;
And then she turned her face
Away and spoke no more.                                             885


*Lancelot*
O mighty Lord, king of heaven,
That's a good and proper token;
By this I must believe you.
Tell me, Reynold is she then dead?


*Reynold*
She is, noble prince,                                               890
And buried in the ground.


*Lancelot here bewails Sandrine and dies*


O Sandrine, you were the branch,
Beautiful with its flowers,
And I was the falcon, I know,
That took away the flower.                                          895

And never since was I joyful,
Since I lost the noble branch!
Always I have suffered,
My most beloved lady!
All the joy that I may see                                    900
On earth is pain for me now,
Mirror above all women
That I ever saw on this earth!
With reason I cry: Alas, Alas,
For the mother who bore me,                                   905
For she rejoiced in her heart
When she gave me her false counsel.
Alas, for the bitter deed,
For the wretched, shameful act!
Alas, that she made me say those words,                       910
By which I lost the lady!
It will cost her and me our lives
For my heart is gnawed by sorrow
And I wish that it were rent
And that my life were done;                                   915
For wherever I may turn,
I will be without joy forever!
The one I chose with true heart
I have lost by bad counsel.
Now my heart has such great sorrow                            920
That it will break with grief.
I hope to see her in Heaven;
For that I will gladly die!
O merciful God in heaven,
Receive now her soul and mine,                                925
For my life is all over.

*Reynold*
Lords and ladies, women and men,
Take an example from this:
Whoever loves in truth,
If he has his will with his love,                                930
Speak about it courteously!
For the noble man of Denmark,
By his bad words and evil counsel,
Was left with the loss
That cost him his noble life.                                    935
And yet he loved the lady
Above all others alive!
He was given false counsel
When he spoke the shameful words
And destroyed his true love,                                     940
So that she slipped away.
Therefore I advise you all
That each man speak courteously
Wherever he may and can,
And especially to the ladies.                                    945
Speak courteously and love truly
And solace will be your reward.
Now I beg you to remain quiet;
Our first play has ended
And we will now play you a farce.                                950

*Note IXC.liii verses*

# THE WITCH

## The Characters

Machtelt
Luutgaert } (three women)
Juliane

# THE WITCH

## HERE BEGINS THE FARCE

*Machtelt*
Alas, good folk, what shall I do?
The wool is better than the yarn;
Everything's going backwards for me
And all is going downhill.
I don't know what's going on:                          5
It must be that foul devil's work
Or I wouldn't be so disturbed!

*Luutgaert*
Now tell me, and don't mince words,
Mechtelt, why are you wailing like that?
I have just chased the fox away                         10
That killed two of my chickens.
And you sit here like that!
Tell me why and give me the truth.

*Machtelt*
Luutgaert, I have good reason!
It's a wonder that I'm not raving!                      15
Bad luck keeps me so down
No matter how I slave day and night
That I'm never getting ahead;
There's magic going on.

*Luutgaert*
By the Virgin Mary, Machtelt,                           20
You're not kidding! I think
I have been bedeviled too,
So that may be your case as well.

My cow has gone dry on me;
She's giving nothing but water.                                    25
Without the help of Hell's tomcat
Or the devil Perlesijn[11]
It wouldn't be like this!
But I do have my suspicions:
Yesterday as I walked by the crossroads                            30
All alone, there I found
An old bitch sitting on the side.
She had some butter before her;
I think she called on the devil
To make that butter appear!                                        35

*Machtelt*
Almighty God, Luutgaert,
I must tell you straight-out:
She had stolen that butter from me!
We should cut her up with knives!
For one month I haven't had                                        40
Any butter from my cow with the blaze;
However I dash and churn,
It's altogether for naught.
By my faith, don't you know her?
Does the shit-whore live near here?                                45

*Luutgaert*
She does, Machtelt, believe me:
In Kortrijk she was born;[12]

---

[11]In medieval Dutch the devil is often portrayed as a tomcat; the origin and meaning of the name *Perlesijn* has not been determined.

[12]Kortrijk is about 47 miles west of Brussels; Ghent (line 51) is about 28 miles northwest of Brussels in modern Belgium.

There they cut off one of her ears
For theft and other crimes.
Shortly thereafter she was banished                    50
From Ghent on peril of the pit!
Many things that she has done
Have left their marks on her.
Don't you know her? It's Juliane;
She lives over there on the corner                      55
With her big book of magic
For all her conjuring tricks.
Too bad she is not deep down
In a pit under the gallows,
Bound fast around her belly!                            60
But now she sells German beer.

*Machtelt*

So what are we waiting for?
If it's Juliane, I know her!
Let's be off to her right now,
Have a pot of beer together.                            65
We must know the truth
About this whole affair!

*Luutgaert*

The sooner the better, Machtelt,
May Saint Bridget bring her disaster!
For much bad luck I suffered                            70
That must have been brought on by her.

*[At Juliane's]*

*Machtelt*
Say, mistress Juliane,
Do you have any German beer?

*Juliane*

Why certainly, mistresses,
What brings you here together?                              75
Well, whatever it may mean
You can always rely on me.

*Lutgaert*

Juliane, we have business here;
We'd like to drink some of your beer.
I beg you, let us sit by the fire                           80
With your beer. We will pay.

*Juliane*

No questions asked, I'll get it;
I am ever at your command

*Machtelt*

Mistress Juliane, we have a problem
And we'd like your advice on that,                          85
But we're afraid of the risk.
You're knowledgeable, we know that;
We would like to get hold of some stuff,
If we knew how to go about it.
People gave us to understand                                90
That, if you were willing,
You could give us a hand with it
And that's why we are here.

*Juliane*

Well, neighbors, if I can help you
With my skill or my advice,                                 95
I would be happy to do so;
Your well-being is my concern!

If you had the hand of a thief[13]
And nine masses read over it,
Things would go well for you,                                    100
Whatever you touched with that hand.


*Luutgaert*
Hey bitch, what you just said
Should give you years of pain!
Now we know out in the open
What you have done to us.                                        105
You'll have to pay us back
Whatever you pilfered from us
Or we'll scratch out your eyes
And hit you so hard with this pot
That your magic will splash from the cracks!                     110


                    *Here they fight*

*Juliane*
Hey you women, don't batter me so hard!


                *CX verses*

---

[13]Popular lore held that there was a connection between theft and magic. In order to have magical powers an object had to be stolen. In several tales a thief's hand could make its owner invisible. Of course, reading masses over a magical object would compound the evil of the black magic.

# THE DEBATE OF WINTER AND SUMMER

## The Characters

Summer
Winter
Lazybones
Handsome
Blabber
Braggart
The Tramp
Venus

# An *Abel* Play of Winter and Summer

## And a Farce to Follow

### *[Prologue]*

Ladies and gentlemen, women and men,
I pray to God the Almighty
That he give us his grace
And eternal life hereafter;
I pray for that in meekness.                                  5
Mark my words and you will hear,
Lords and ladies all around,
How Winter and Summer do battle—
And the qualities of these two.
Be silent and make no sound;                                 10
Mark my words how it begins.
I beg you to pay attention,
For it is rare and also noble
In respect to their words and replies,
Both of Summer and of Winter.                                15
Summer is on his way
So know that he is coming.
Be quiet and make no noise,
I beg you kindly, all of you,
And I commend you to our heavenly Father.                    20

*Summer*
I am Summer and I make the birds
Sing their songs, make the flowers bud
And the green leaves in the forest;
I take away Winter's chill
And bring us the sweet season                                 25

And cause everyone to play
With his sweetheart in great joy,
When they see the flowers bloom
That were hidden in Winter time.
I bring so many sweet morrows                    30
With dew at time of dawn!
When you go out with your sweetheart
Playing in the valley of love
O, you will have such joy,
Picking flowers at dawn.                          35

*Winter*
Shut up, you fool, keep quiet!
I am Winter that holds all in check:
The birds that sing in summer—
I can make them all fall silent,
I have them all in my control.                    40
When I do as I am wont
And the wind cuts from the East
I cause everyone's teeth to chatter
And make them slap their arms,
And their fingers crack in the cold.              45
I make the pigs squeal out
Along the streets and the roads.[14]
You'd better stop your bragging
For I've everything in my power:
I rob the birds of their song                     50
And subdue the animals all;
The fish in the rivers as well—
I lock them up under the ice.

---

[14] Pigs roamed around freely in the streets in the Middle Ages.

*Summer*

Sir Winter, I know it well;

You have a cruel nature                                    55

And you are so cold-blooded

That many shiver with fear

Who're full of joy in Summer.

If I follow my inclination

Then all forget the sorrows                                60

That they felt during the Winter;

I make all those live in joy

That you had held cooped up.

When the flowers burst to bloom

Then all know that Summer has come,                        65

And many people love me

That hate you for being grim.


*Winter*

I know very well, Sir Summer,

That many do not love me:

The people who have spent all                              70

Their pennies in the tavern,

Who love to drink and gamble

So they can't afford any clothing!

In the Summer they lie in the sun

And think it will last forever.                            75

Then when I come with my downpours

Bringing hail and icy snow,

Then I bring them such pain

That their guts shiver with cold.

The people who loll and laze                               80

And rely too much on you—

Now they shiver by the road;

Though they might be young and noble

I can hold all those under control,

Who didn't save their coins.                                    85

*Summer*

Sir Winter, you are so harsh!

It often shows in your face;

But I am much surprised

That you will stand against me:

All the world is on my side!                                    90

Noble I am by nature;

I fill the barns and stores

And make the crops grow;

I bring the sweet warm weather—

That's my nature as the Summer.                                 95

I make the orchards bloom

That stand all bare in winter.

*Winter*

That's why I am on top—

Because I control all things.

You cannot demonstrate                                          100

That I am not lord over you.

*Lazybones*

By God, Sir Winter, that's right!

For whatever Summer makes grow

You can eat it all with ease

While you sit by the fire—                                      105

Drinking your good beer,

Eating bread, wine, meat and fish—

Have it put on your plate

While you sit there, drunk as a cow.

It's so cold out in the street                                  110

That no one can stand the cold.
What Summer works to produce,
Winter consumes it altogether.
If you want to tell the truth:
Summer is only a slave!                                115
Those hot days are so long
I'm exhausted by the work;
I'm tired of those long days
And praise Winter as my lord.

*Handsome*
Lazybones, you are a fool                               120
To be so harsh towards Summer,
Who all the time brings about
Good cheer, amusement and joy;
Brings kisses to many lips—
Summer does, hidden in the green.                       125
You can't do that in winter!
When the flowers bloom in the valley
And birds sing their song—
Each after his own nature—
Then there is no creature on earth                      130
Who doesn't rejoice in that;
Lords and ladies, women and men,
Their hearts open up in joy.
When sweet Summer time comes around
With his flowers and sweet herbs                        135
And the birds begin to sing
Then he brings the game of Love
That's played in hidden spots
Where the flowers scent the air.
All those things we lack in Winter                      140
Because he is so fierce.

*Blabber*
Here I am, my name is Blabber,
And I will tell the whole truth.
By God in heaven I swear
That my lord Winter as well                              145
Favors the game of Love
That you are talking about.
When two lovers are in bed,
Naked under the covers,
They are having a joyful time,                           150
Even though the birds do not sing.
The nights are cold and long,
And the cold makes them huddle close,
Their legs about each other.
Sir Winter compels them to that                         155
And brings all the fun about
When they play the game of Love.
I tell you without dissembling—
For I know the truth about it—
In summer the nights are so hot:                        160
One lies here and the other there;
They dare not come too close
Because of the heat of the season,
But in winter they press side to side
And stick to each other's bush.                         165

*Winter*
By God, Blabber, you have spoken
The truth and done it well!
I would hardly at any time
Disturb the game of Love;
I see so many red lips                                   170
Kissing in those long nights;

When two lovers lie and sleep
On a comfortable bed
And give each other pleasure,
That's just as much Love's game,                    175
Though it is not in a garden
Where the birds are singing!

*Braggart*
Sir Winter, you'd like to subdue
The Summer, but it won't be!
It would sooner cost me my life                     180
Than that I'd tolerate that.
You bring us nothing but cold,
Rain, hail and coldest snow;
You cause such pain to many
That they forget all joy.                           185
Sir Summer, on the other hand,
Fills every man's heart full of joy
Who is a wretch all winter,
Lying in the ashes by the fire.
No way I can find that you                          190
Would not end up bottommost.

*Winter*
Sir Braggart, it surprises me
That you take such a high tone;
Really, you cannot maintain
That I must not be most important.                  195
I rob Summer of his hot glow,
And I obstruct the clear skies;
I also consume all the crops
That the Summer can bring forth.
There's no woman or man on earth                    200

Who doesn't need to be in my employ;
I'm ready to do battle
To see who will be on top.

*Handsome*
No longer can I hold my tongue
And suppress the truth about this!                    205
Sir Winter, with hunger you'd starve
Were it not for noble Sir Summer.
Blessed Winter, what would you do
If Summer did not in his mercy
At all times bring forth                              210
Bread and wine for you to live?
All else that we have in the world
Summer produces for us:
Apples, pears and other fruit
That all the world lives on.                          215
If you had wisdom and good sense
You'd bow your head low to him.

*Blabber*
Sir Handsome you must talk no more,
Sir Winter is too strong for you.
If I look at you carefully                            220
I note your lips are blue with cold.
By God, you are nowise warm
And heat is far from you!
You are not feeling warm, I see,
Although you spoke in such high tone.                 225

*Summer*
By God, Sir Winter, I'll have revenge
That you permit such high-toned speech!

When the flowers are out in the valley
And blossom and smell so sweet,
When the sun in the heavens                              230
Shines its joyful way,
And we find no thing on this earth
That doesn't bloom or bear fruit—
Sir Winter, your life is at risk then
And you will lose your strength.                          235

*Braggart*
And when the sweet night arrives
With its dew in yonder dale,
When the nightingale is singing
And the flowers stand out in the green—
White and red, each as is his nature—                    240
When the fruit trees are blooming,
And everyone's heart floats in joy,
Then Love multiplies in joy's realm.

*Winter*
I never heard such marvels before!
You speak just as if I would keep                         245
Love subdued—I'm surprised to hear—
And it doesn't exist in Winter.
I will be very clear about that:
People love just as well in Winter
And there is a much nobler love                           250
Than in Summer, know that well;
Though the dew may not be as sweet
Understand: The nights are long,
Giving each a chance to talk;
Whenever there are two lovers                             255
Each lovingly in the arms

Of his own beloved,
When they warm each other then
As the cold urges them to do,
There may be no nightingale singing                     260
But the game of Love is played
More often than in Summer;
I will pledge my life to that.


*Summer*
And I'll jump into battle myself,
Though I may suffer hurt for that.                       265
The gladder season, the gladder heart;
The gladder heart, the more loving.
When we have the Summer season
And the flowers are opening up
And the little birds sing loudly,                        270
Then all hearts are vivacious,
For the Summer is so gracious
And so noble in its nature.
A man's heart might be angry and crabbed
But when Summer comes to the land                        275
All joys reveal themselves
That were subdued in Winter.
People as well as the birds
Do not sing during the Winter;
They must all remain indoors.                            280
When it freezes or they are snowed in
Many wish they weren't living
Because of this deprivation,
But the Summer brings them joy
When they feel the bright sunshine.                      285
Sir Winter, you must yield yourself
Convinced, admit the truth.

*Winter*

You must sing another tune
For me to say I'm convinced!
We're so strong, I and my party,                                    290
That I will make many shiver.
Would I give myself in surrender?
May God curse me if I did!
I have them all in my control
That live under the sky.                                            295
But in honor of Venus and her crown,
And because she is Lady of Love,
And you want to convince me that love
Is better pursued in Summer
And that it declines in Winter,                                     300
Therefore I will cross swords
To prove that you are lying.
Set your life against mine—
To be decided in twenty-four hours—
That love is more noble                                             305
In time of Winter, for sure,
Than in Summer time, let it be known!
On this I will bear the palm
For Venus, Lady of Love;
For her sake I will start the battle;                               310
Take up my glove if you are a man.

*Summer*

I was never in better spirits
Than I am at this hour!
Joy and happiness I will bring
To so many living beings.                                           315
Now it has come to this point
That I will do battle with you,

I will bring such shame on you—
I will take your life from you
And so drive you away;                                    320
It will be Summer forever!

*The Tramp*
I'm glad in my heart for this;
Sir Summer, pay him back in his coin!
Sir Winter, you've been so fierce
That I've been scared to talk.                            325
I know about your tricks;
You've caused me such misery.
Now I praise Summer and his protection
For he gladdens my heart
And that of other tramps                                  330
Who are toasting themselves by the fire.
Now Summer comes with his mercy
To chase you out of here.
You forced me to sit by the fire,
In the ashes like a roasting hen;                         335
That's why I must love Summer,
Who will chase you away.
You've caused me such disaster
To sit in the ashes by the fire;
Sir Winter, you must go away!                             340
You've been here too long.
You made me sit in the stench
And the smoke, it seems to me;
That's why I give my love to him,
To Summer, who will take your life.                       345

*Winter*
Get out of here, filthy wretch
With your foolhardy talk!

I'll bring such disgrace to you
That you'll be sorry you are alive.
I'll make you shiver with cold,                              350
Burn the marrow out of your legs.
Filthy wretch, get away from here!
You must be cooped up in your nest.
Sir Summer, I say loud and clear:
You must appoint a guarantor                                 355
So I may come without worry
To do battle with you.


*The Tramp*
So truly may God damn me,
I'll be one of his guarantors!
I love him with all my heart,                                360
Noble Summer, the brave hero.
I put up my land as assurance,
As well as my life and goods,
That he will come in great spirits
To fight against you, Sir Winter.                            365


*Blabber*
Shut up, you! Who wants you here?
In the devil's name, get away
And sit down by the fire!
You seem to be so cold,
You must be all out of clothes.                              370
You truly are a real tramp;
You must've been to some fine market
And sold everything you had.
What devil brought you here?
You seem to be a real vagabond.                              375
In the Summer you'd be all right,
I can see that from your outfit;

It seems to me—if you had money—
You'd gamble it straight away.
Friend, you are not respected here;    380
You must stand aside.

*The Tramp*
Yea, boy, if I had good clothes
You'd all snuggle up to me;
But now I'm made out for a tramp
Because I am not dressed well.    385
That's how I lead my life:
Among the scoundrels and tramps,
More likely to have a louse
Than a coat of scarlet stuff.
But if fierce Winter were dead    390
My heart would much rejoice.
May God grant triumph to Summer
So that he may win the fight.

*Handsome*
Sir Winter, according to rule,
I will be a surety for him;    395
I will warrant that the high baron
Will appear here like a lion
To uphold his honor in battle.
Sir Winter, since you are the challenger
Fulfill now the battle conditions.    400

*Blabber*
I wish that Sir Winter be honored
And I'll be his warrant right now,
That he will appear as a warrior
To fulfill what has been started.

May God grant him everything good 405
So that he remain in his honor.
Now hurry up, all, and leave;
Sir Winter shall prepare himself.

*[All off, except Handsome]*

*Handsome*
O God, who will manage to settle
The dispute between these two lords? 410
All the world will be brought to ruin
If Summer is overcome;
And also if Winter is cut down
One quarter of the year is lost!
Great harm will result from this, 415
Whoever is overcome.
Alas, I don't know what to do—
How can this thing be stopped?
For they're both so determined
And have sworn such solemn oaths— 420
There is no one born on earth
Who has power to restrain them.
But it has just occurred to me
That I could go cheerfully
To Venus, the dear goddess. 425
She is lady above them all:
I hope she will prevent it.
If I tell her and make it known
To Venus the noble lady
How this matter has developed, 430
I know she will not hold back
But will settle their dispute.
Now I'll run as fast as I can

To Venus, my dear Lady.
If we'd lose Summer and his sunshine                      435
All joy would be lost as well.

            *[While speaking, Handsome has moved to Venus' realm]*

Where are you high-born Lady,
Noble Queen Venus?

*Venus*
Tell me, friend, in kindly manner,
Wherefore have you come here?                             440

*Handsome*
I tell you Lady, loud and clear:
It's for two noble lords
Who swore to each other's death
And challenged each other to battle
Tomorrow before the hour of Vespers;                     445
They've sworn to kill each other.
There is none on earth so great
That he can take on this conflict—
Lord or lady, woman or man—
Except you alone, dear Lady!                              450
These lords are mighty and great:
One is Summer, rich in possessions,
The other Winter, equally so.
They fell into a dispute;
For your sake, noble Lady,                                455
These things have come about.
They will never be settled
Unless you do it yourself.

*Venus*
Dear friend, now explain to me:
How has this come about?                                              460
You say it has happened through me,
But I'm innocent of it all.

*Handsome*
Lady, I wish you to understand:
They quarreled with angry words,
With many around who heard them—                                     465
How they called each other names;
And each put forward his reasons
For his actions and his power!
Then Summer spoke loud and clear
That he was handsome and gracious                                    470
And that he made all vivacious
In their hearts, and full of joy;
And that we find, in Summer time,
A nobler kind of love
Than what is found in Winter;                                        475
Noble Lady, those were his words.
Then angry Winter stepped forward,
And he was incensed and grim;
He took out his glove
And challenged Summer to fight.                                      480
And Summer rushed eagerly
To the glove and picked it up
And intends to do battle with him;
They have sureties on both sides.
Noble Lady, stop the fighting                                        485
For you have the power for that!
The Winter is fierce and strong:
I fear for my Lord Summer.

*Venus*

Friend, I will make good haste
And be there early tomorrow                          490
Before the sun has risen.
I will be there in good time,
Before the lords start their battle;
I will take it up on both sides.
If we allow the lords to fight                       495
Much dismay would be the result:
Whichever of them would lose,
The world would be brought to ruin.
I will take up this dispute
If I have the power for it.                           500

*Handsome*

Noble Lady, now I will turn
Back home in joyful mood;
You will turn it all to the best;
I know that for a truth.
There is no one on this earth                         505
Who can end it as you can.

*Venus*

Friend, I will be there
Tomorrow, before the sun's up.

*[Venus off]*

*Handsome*

That seemed the best plan to me;
It is better that it be resolved,                     510
For if one of them would be killed
It would be cause of great sorrow;

But if my Lord Summer would die,
Then we would all fare badly:
Winter would not spare us—                                          515
He is altogether fierce!

### [The Next Morning]

*Winter*
Now here I am on my way
To the battle, as befits me;
Here I call Sir Summer forth
To come and defend his honor.                                       520

*Summer*
Sir Winter, there's no need at all
To think that I will not appear!
That's why I accepted the fight,
So that I may take your life.

*The Tramp*
May God, who is Lord above all,                                     525
Give victory to you, Sir Summer,
So that you may take Winter's life!
Then I would rejoice in my heart;
He causes me so much pain
That my liver shivers with cold.                                    530

### [Venus appears]

*Venus*
Lordings, I pray you give up
This disputation and battle:
You are brothers to each other;

It seems to me 'twould be unseemly
To engage each other in battle,                                       535
Where one might kill the other.
Sir Summer, please leave this to me,
I pray you, for the sake of true love.

*Summer*
Lady Venus, noble Queen,
I don't really like to do that.                                       540
Nonetheless I will not refuse you,
Because you are Lady of Love,
So I will yield the battle to you—
Do with it as you desire.
There is no one alive on this earth                                   545
Who could get me to yield but you.

*Venus*
Sir Summer, I owe you my thanks
For this forevermore.
Now I pray you here, Sir Winter,
That you act the same way towards me.                                 550

*Winter*
Lady Venus, you wear the crown
And are the Lady of Love;
Therefore I wouldn't know how
To deny you what you desire.
Lady Venus, you have my respect                                       555
And I gladly submit to you.

*Venus*
Then you will never quarrel from now on
And eternally be brothers.

God, who made water and wine[15]
And all that we find in the world—                              560
He made the firmament,
Set the seven planets therein
And the twelve signs as well;
These rule over all the world:
They make it hot and cold;                                       565
They bring about Winter and Summer,
As the astronomers teach us.
One is cold and the other is hot,
And this will never stop:
It must be either Winter or Summer;                              570
Sometimes the hot sunshine,
Sometimes hail and cold snow.
This will never come to an end.
As long as the world will last
Each will work after his own nature                              575
For God has ordained it like that.
If either one is hindered—
Summer or Winter as well—
Everything on this earth
Would perish and disappear                                       580
As if time would stand still.
One cannot be without the other.

*Winter*
Lady Venus, you've won me over
For your words are fully true:
I must follow upon Summer                                        585
And Summer must follow me.

---

[15]This line is rather puzzling. One would expect 'wine from water' (as in the Wedding at Cana, John 2).

*Summer*

I know that as well as you do—
That one can't be without the other,
But my pain and my complaint
Are that you would dislodge me                        590
When I spoke, and told me to shut up!
And you said you were the tyrant;
Sir Winter, I know full well
That you are the tyrant of those
Whom I cause to live in joy                            595
When I come with my flowers.


*Venus*

Lordings, I have reconciled
This dispute between you two
By your wish and your consent
That I should give my opinion.                         600
Now be silent on this all
And you will be brothers forever.
Let us eat and drink wine
And live in joy and peace.


*[All off, except the Tramp]*


*The Tramp*

Aye, now I must all my life                            605
Be under Winter's rod,
Who gives me so much misery
That I don't know what to do.
No thanks I owe to Venus
The queen, when she came here                          610
And settled these two's dispute.
The devil brought her here

Just when I was so overjoyed
That Winter would be chased out!
Summer would have taken his life                    615
For he was so confident
And his weapons were so good
And his sword so well sharpened
He would surely have beaten him
If they had come to battle.                          620
But Lady Venus has reconciled them!
My heart is sad about that.
Now I'll run off like a pig
To Maastricht by the coalmines;[16]
There will I stay in the poorhouse                   625
Until Summer comes to the land.

*Nota vic.xxv verses*

---

[16]Maastricht is a town in the province of Limburg in the southern part of the
Netherlands. In the fourteenth century it was part of the Duchy of Brabant. From
as early the twelfth century, coal was mined in the vicinity of Maastricht by the
Abbey of Rolduc.

# RUBEN

## The Characters

Ruben
The Wife, Ruben's mother-in-law
Gosen, Ruben's father-in-law

# RUBEN

## HERE BEGINS THE FARCE

*Ruben*
Hey boy, I know very well
And am fully aware of the fact
That many rush into action
And afterwards have their regrets.
Here I am, married to a young wife                          5
Since about three months ago,
And last night when I came home
She was delivered of a child!
And yet I've always been told
That it normally takes nine months!                        10
Nonetheless all who saw the child
Say that he seemed to lack nothing:
A fully developed creature,
All his limbs were perfectly formed,
Nails and toes all fully shaped.                           15
Did this happen in three months?
No one alive can tell me
That I have fathered that child.
She must have started this long
Before I took her for a wife.                              20
Cursed be the devil that I took her!
But her mother left me no peace—
By God, she knew what was up
Better than I did, I'm sure.

*The Wife [Ruben's mother-in-law]*
What, Ruben, is that you?                                  25
Now tell me, how is my daughter?

*184*

*Ruben*

Indeed ma'am, I don't know:
Your daughter just had a child;
A proper young fellow she had—
He could have been six months old.                                30

*The Wife*

Thank God for that many times
That she got through that all right!

*Ruben*

I am not so well pleased with the fact
That she was in such great haste.
I am so beside myself                                             35
That I do not know what to think.

*The Wife*

How and in what manner?
Don't fear, tell me what you think.
I will give you such advice
That you'll be fully satisfied.                                   40

*Ruben*

Indeed, if they would kill me
I couldn't be more displeased;
For it is on this very day
Three months since I took your daughter
And first had dealings with her—                                 45
Give or take another five nights.
Now she brought a child in the world
That could well be six months old:
Not as much as one hair is lacking
Or nails on fingers or toes;                                      50

It has been carried to term
More or less nine months, to the full—
I dare well say it out loud:
That child cannot be mine.

*The Wife*
Jeez, listen to this man!                                    55
I swear you are out of your mind.

*Ruben*
I am neither tipsy nor tight;
I know full well what I say:
If I put one and two together[17]
It makes three months and five nights.                      60

*The Wife*
My dear fellow, you're way out of line:
You've remembered the time all wrong!
You deserve to be accused
That you cry shame upon your wife.
Three months before and three after                          65
And three months in between—
That's still nine months altogether;
I know that for a fact.

*Ruben*
If you can explain that to me
You can call me a bright guy.[18]                            70

---

[17]It is likely that Ruben here counts on his fingers and that the mother-in-law does the same thing in presenting her calculations to him in the following lines.

[18]The text has "call me Hugh." The name Hugo means 'wit, intellect' (see Stellinga, ed., p. 76).

I remember it so exactly
Because of the cow that I sold then
And the money was brought in last night;
When the man wanted to buy it
He asked me to give him credit—  75
Three months was the term we set.
What do you think—I'm a fool,
That I have no idea of the time?

*The Wife*
I can hear that you are all besotted
For three times three does still make nine.  80
Here's my husband, our daughter's father;
I know that he knows it as well.
Hey, Gosen, are you at hand?
Come here, I must talk to you.

*Gosen*
Jeez, what the devil do you need?  85
Here I am, what do you want?

*The Wife*
Now tell me, dear husband Gosen:
Remember that our daughter was wed?

*Gosen*
For sure, and she married a man—
'Tis about three months ago.  90

*The Wife*
It is, on this very day,
Nine months, if you count them right;
But Ruben, our son, is dismayed

That she has just born him a child.
If it were only seven months                                    95
That could have happened quite well.

*Gosen*
Well! Ruben, dear son, I didn't see you.
So our daughter gave birth, God preserve her!

*Ruben*
Yes, but I cannot comprehend
That I could be the father!                                      100
I can swear by my good faith
That I had her no more than three months.

*The Wife*
And three months that she was your bride,
And three months that you didn't count.
If you put those all together                                   105
Then it is nine months withal,
And that is the proper term
For a woman to carry a child.

*Gosen*
It is the truth she is telling you!
In this she did not lie.                                         110

*Ruben*
Did the devil fool me then
When I remember it by my cow?
I want to say something more:
When I took your daughter as my wife,
And first came to sleep with her,                               115
And I wanted to set her to work—

Pardon ma'am, I must tell you this—
She knew as much about it as I!
She arranged her body just so—
As if she had seven years practice!                     120
I took that for a poor sign;
I held my tongue but I was cross.


*Gosen*
That's just like her mother when we married
And together got into bed.
She knew just as much about it                           125
As if I'd had her for seven months!


*The Wife*
You want to know why that was?
I had learned it all from hearsay!
If someone tries really hard
And remembers what he is told                            130
He will never be lacking in skill.
That's how it was with my daughter.
Listen, friend, don't be dismayed!
Do you want to understand?
The nighttimes slipped away from you                     135
And you didn't count them in
When you dallied in pleasure
With my daughter, your good wife,
And lay with her sweet body
Cozy under the covers,                                   140
Each in the other's arms.
That time you forgot about,
But you did count all the days
When you saw the sun appear.
In every woman that's with child                         145

It grows both nights and days.
That's the truth and no fable;
That's why you lost track of that time.
If you want me to swear to the truth
I will swear it on a cross:                                      150
When my daughter came to your house
She knew no more about men,
Nor ever had thought about them,
Than I did when I married her father!

*Gosen*

By God, I was pretty cross though,                              155
When you did such an expert job!
I thought: This one got a blast
Somewhere from a couple of fellows;
But you gave me to understand
That you knew it from hearsay only.                             160

*Ruben*

Indeed, sir, I've heard it said:
Women's skill is hard to fathom!
But if I had found your daughter
A bungler instead of a whiz . . .
What the devil, she was so skilled                              165
That I could not be more surprised.

*The Wife*

That's because she wanted to please you
And had a great liking for you!
She was always smiling for joy
Whenever she saw you around.                                    170
The first thing she always said
Was: "If I've seen my sweet Ruben

The day cannot go wrong."
That was always her refrain.
'Twas great affection that moved her;                    175
That's why she couldn't pretend.
You don't even have to worry
That my daughter was a virgin, for sure,
Five years after she was born.
I swear by the relics to that!                           180

*Ruben*
By God, I'd be sorry forever
If I had caused her pain;
But that I lost track of the time
Is something I can't comprehend,
For I always had the feeling                             185
That it was only three months ago.

*The Wife*
Listen, dear, to make you happy
I will set it out right for you
And count the time on these three fingers:
The first three months I put here;                       190
The next three months she sat by the fire;
And the third three months are the nights:
So that's the whole time complete
And nine months altogether!
By the relics, the child has a father—                   195
Don't think otherwise anymore.

*Gosen*
She speaks the truth, by God—
She cannot lie about that!

*Ruben*

Am I letting the devil cheat me?
Did I forget to count the nights?                    200
And torment my heart for nothing?
Then the fault is completely mine.
I'd be sorry for this forever
If I had reproached my wife.
Now I'll go make her something to eat           205
And show her some respect
And thank our dear Lord God
That he brought me such a fine child.

*The Wife*

Do, and hurry as much as you can
And put a pot of meat on the fire,                 210
For I'll come visit you soon
And see how she is doing.

*Ruben*

I'll be happy to do that, God knows,
And I will make it so good
And it will taste so delicious                          215
That you'll lick your fingers after.

### [Ruben off]

*The Wife*

That's how you must deal with these blockheads,
If you have to have such a man.
Put a blue hood on his head
And stick it into a bag.[19]                              220

---

[19]"To put a blue hood on the husband" is a well-known expression for making
him a cuckold. It is illustrated in Brueghel's painting of the Netherlandish Proverbs
(Berlin, Staatliche Museen). See W. S. Gibson, *Bruegel* (New York, 1993),

*Gosen*

You and your daughter are trollops:
You'd gull Ruben any time.
I suspected such things as well
When you disabused me like that.

*The Wife*

I bet you never noticed a thing                                 225
That you'd not be embarrassed to say.

*Gosen*

You know so many sly tricks!
Whatever I see you'll deny,
Just like you did with Ruben
And counted him nine for three                                 230
And explained it to him so well:
He didn't know what to say.
You and your kind can twist around
And hoodwink many a man
That married many a wife                                       235
And thought she was a virgin,
But she was rammed in the bush!
Just like you were when I took you;
And when our daughter started with Ruben
She certainly knew what was what!                              240

*The Wife*

Are you wagging your tongue again?
I thank the devil for that
And right now I'll slug your face

---

pl. 40 and 44. "To stick someone's head into a bag" may mean something like "to shut him up" (Stellinga; ed., p. 85).

So your teeth come out of your mouth!

*Gosen*
But I will make you sing first.[20]                                      245

*Nota iic.xlv verses*

---

[20]Presumably, he will make her cry with pain because he is beating her.

# APPENDIX

The following extract provides a representative passage from an *abel* play and its accompanying farce. It is intended to provide the reader with an opportunity to compare the English translation with the language of the original Middle Dutch text.

The photograph on the facing page shows folio 178 recto of the Van Hulthem manuscript (Brussels, Royal Library Albert I, Manuscript 15.589–623), provided by kind permission of the Royal Library. The text on this page is the end of *Esmoreit* (beginning with Platus' speech at line 983) and the beginning of *Lippin*. After the Young Man's four lines, the stage directions note the hanging of Robbrecht, followed by the Young Man's epilogue. The passage concludes with an *Amen* and the line count of the play (1008 verses). This is followed by another epilogue spoken by Platus (probably added at a later stage), admonishing the audience to remain seated for the farce. The epilogue to *Esmoreit* ends with the fourth line of the second column.

After a blank double line space, one finds the heading for the farce ("Here begins the farce") followed by its number in the manuscript (170) indicated in roman numerals. After three more blank line spaces, one sees the rubric "Here begins the wife." There is no list of the characters in the farce (or for any of the other plays in the manuscript). Each heading for a new speaker is preceded by a paragraph mark, as is the first line of each speech. The contents of the entire page are transcribed below. Line numbers have been added corresponding to those of the translation.

Ghi soutten hebben doot ghesteken
En haddi mi niet hoeren spreken
Daer ic ten aenganghe quam gerede                    [985]

Ic en was nie soe wel te vreden
Als dat icken jeghen u cochte om gelt
Ic gaeft u al onghetelt
In een foertsier was yvorijn
Noch soude ment vinden in uwe scrijn        [990]
Daer willic onder setten mijn lijf

De jonghelinc

Aye mi robberecht fel keitijf
Met rechten ic u wel haten mach
Ghi selt nu hebben uwen doems dach
Al die werelt en holpe u niet        [995]

Robbrecht hanctmen hier
De jonghelinc noch

Al dus eest menechwerf gesciet
Quade werken comen te quaden loene
Maer reine herten spannen croene
Die vol doeghden sijn ende vol trouwen
Daer omme radic heren ende vrouwen        [1000]
Dat ghi u herte in doeghden stelt
So werdi in dinde met gode verseilt
Daer boven inden hoghen troene
Daer die inghelen singhen scoene
Dies onne ons die hemelsche vader        [1005]
Ny segt Amen alle gader

Amen .xc. viii. verse
De meester

God die nemen ons allen in hoeden
Nu hoert ghi wise ende ghi vroede
Hier soe moghdi merken ende verstaen
Hoe esmoreit ene wrake heeft gedaen        [1010]
Over robbrecht sinen neve al hier te stede
Elc blive sittene in sinen vrede
Niemen en wille thuus weert gaen
Ene sotheit sal men u spelen gaen
Die cort sal sijn doe ic u weten        [1015]

Wie hongher heeft hi mach gaen eten
Ende gaet alle dien graet neder
Ghenoeghet u soe comt alle mergen weder
      Hier beghint die sotternie
       .c.lxx
       Hier beghint dwijf
Hem segt hem god hebs al deel
Ic wil gaen driven mijn riveel
Met minen suete lieve int gras
Hets lanc leden dat ic met hem niet en was
Hem segt hem waer sidi lippijn           [5]


       Lippijn
Ic ben hier wat saelt sijn
        Sijn wijf
Lippijn ghi moet gaen halen borre ende vier
Ende ic sal weder comen scier
Ende bringhen ons iet dat wi selen eten
        Lippijn
Bider doot ons heren ghi selet vergeten       [10]
Ghi pleeght soe dicwile lange te merren
        Sijn wijf
Wat lippijn ghi en moghet u niet erren
Want ic hebbe dicwile vele te doene
Eer ic ghehoere mine sermoene
Soe vallet hoghe op den dach          [15]
Ende eer ic ten vleeschuus comen mach
Soe copic oec gherne goeden coep
Dan soe moetic beiden tot den loep

# BIBLIOGRAPHY

## EDITIONS

Dijk, H. van, ed., *Lanseloet van Denemerken, een abel spel*. Amsterdam: Amsterdam University Press, 1995.

Dijk, H. van, F. Kramer, and J. Tersteeg, eds. *Die Buskenblaser*, in H. van Dijk, W. P. Gerritsen, Orlanda S. H. Lie, and F. van der Poel, eds., *Klein Kapitaal uit het Handschrift-Van-Hulthem*. Hilversum: Verloren, 1992. Pages 164–79.

Duinhoven, A. M. *Die Sotternie van Lippijn*, in H. van Dijk, W. P. Gerritsen, Orlanda S. H. Lie and F. van der Poel, eds., *Klein Kapitaal uit het Handschrift-Van-Hulthem*. Hilversum: Verloren, 1992. Pages 122–38.

*Een Seer Ghenoechlike ende Amoroeze Historie vanden Eedelen Lantsloet ende die Scone Sandrijn.* Facsimile of the c. 1486 edition by G. van Ghemen. The Hague: Nijhoff, 1902.

Hoffmann von Fallersleben, H. *Horae Belgicae*. Vol. 6. Breslau: Aderholz, 1838.

Hüsken, W. N. M., and F. A. M. Schaars, eds. *Sandrijn en Lanslot: Diplomatische Uitgave van Twee Toneelrollen uit het Voormalig Archief van de Rederijkerskamer De Fiolieren te 's-Gravenpolder*. Nijmegen-Grave: Alfa, 1985.

Kammen, L. van, ed. *De Abele Spelen*. Amsterdam: Athenaeum-Polak & van Gennep, 1968.

Leendertz, P., ed. *Middelnederlandse Dramatische Poëzie*. Bibliotheek van Middelnederlandsche Letterkunde. Leiden: Sijthoff, 1899–1907.

Moltzer, H. E., ed. *De Middelnederlandsche Dramatische Poëzie*. Groningen: Wolters, 1868–75.

Roemans, R., and R. Gaspar, eds. *Een Abel Spel van Gloriant*. Antwerpen: Nederlandse Boekhandel, 1956.

———. *Esmoreit*. Antwerpen: Nederlandse Boekhandel, 1954.

Roemans, R., and H. van Assche, eds. *Een Abel Spel van Lanseloet van Denemerken*. 2nd ed. Amsterdam: Nederlandse Boekhandel, 1966.

Stellinga, G., ed. *Het Abel Spel 'Vanden Winter ende Vanden Somer' ende ene Sotternie 'Rubben' Navolghende: Voorafgegaan door de Fragmenten ene Sotte Boerde 'Drie Daghe Here' ende ene Goede Sotternie 'Truwanten.'* 2nd ed. Zutphen: Thieme, 1975.

Vromans, J., ed. *Die Hexe*, in H. van Dijk, W. P. Gerritsen, Orlanda S. H. Lie, and F. van der Poel, eds., *Klein Kapitaal uit het Handschrift-Van-Huthem*. Hilversum: Verloren, 1992. Pages 180–89.

Werkgroep Brusselse en Utrechtse Neerlandici, eds. *Truwanten: een Toneeltekst uit het Handschrift-Van Hulthem*. Groningen: Wolters-Noordhoff, 1978.

## TRANSLATIONS

Ayres, H. M. *An Ingenious Play of Esmoreit, the King's Son of Sicily*. Introduction by A. Barnouw. The Hague: Nijhoff, 1924.

Colledge, E. "A Fine Play of Lancelot, How He Came to Woo a Damsel Who Was in His Mother's Service." In *Reynard the Fox and Other Mediaeval Netherlands Secular Literature*. London: Heinemann; New York: London House and Maxwell, 1967.

Decker, Theresa, and Martin Walsh. "Three *Sotterniën*: Farcical Afterpieces from the Hulthem Manuscript." *Dutch Crossings* 48 (1992): 73–96.

Geyl, P. *A Beautiful Play of Lancelot of Denmark: How He Fell in Love with a Lady Who Waited upon his Mother*. The Hague: Nijhoff; London: Gyldendal, 1924.

Oakshott, J. and E. Strietman. *Esmoreit: An Excellent Play of Esmoreit, Prince of Sicily*. In *Dutch Crossings* 30 (1986): 3–39.

Vroom, Theresia de. *Netherlandic Secular Plays from the Middle Ages; the "Abele Speleny" and the Farces of the Hulthem Manuscript*. Carleton Renaissance Plays in Translation 29. Ottawa: Dovehouse Editions, 1997.

## CRITICISM

Abeele, Baudouin van de. *La Fauconnerie dans les Lettres Françaises du XIIe au XIVe Siecle*. Mediaevalia Lovaniensia I, xviii. Leuven: Leuven University Press, 1990.

Andreas Capellanus. *Andreas Capellanus on Love*. Ed. and trans., P. G. Walsh. London: Duckworth, 1982.

Anrooij, W. van. "Bijdrage tot een Geografische Situering van het Handschrift Van Hulthem." *Spiegel der Letteren* 28, 4 (1986): 225–33.

———. "29 September 1399: In Brussel vinden twee Mirakelen Plaats, die kort daarop in het Handschrift Van Hulthem Worden Opgeschreven—Literaire Veelzijdigheid in een Stedelijke Verzamelcodex." *Nederlandse Literatuur, een Geschiedenis*. Ed. M. A. Schenkeveld-van der Dussen et al. Groningen: Nijhoff, 1993. Pages 86–91.

Anrooij, W. van, and A. M. J. van Buuren. "'s Levens Felheid in een Band: Het Handschrift-Van Hulthem." *Op Belofte van Profijt*. Ed. Herman Pleij. Amsterdam: Prometheus, 1991. Pages 184–99.

Anrooij, W. van, and R. Sleiderink. "Averne, Auvergne en Navarra: Over de Betekenis van Geografische Aanduiding." *Spiegel der Letteren*, 38, 2–3 (1996): 185–88.

Aubailly, J. C. *Le Monologue, le Dialogue et la Sottie: Essai sur Quelques Genres Dramatiques de la Fin du Moyen Age et du Début du XVIe Siècle*. Paris: H. Champion, 1976.

Bal, Mieke. *Verkrachting Verbeeld: Seksueel Geweld in Cultuur Gebracht*. Utrecht: HES, 1988.

Beidler, Peter G., and Therese Decker. "*Lippijn*: A Middle Dutch Source for the *Merchant's Tale?*" *The Chaucer Review* 23, 3 (1989): 236–50.

Besamusca, B. "*Amor hereos* in Middle Dutch Literature: The Case of Lancelot of Denmark." *Literary Aspects of Courtly Culture: Selected Papers of the Seventh Congress of the International Courtly Literature Society*. Ed. Donald Maddox and Sara Sturm-Maddox. Woodbridge/Rochester: Boydell and Brewer, 1994. Pages 189–96.

Besamusca, B. and Orlanda S. H. Lie. "The Prologue to 'Arturs Doet'." *Medieval Dutch Literature in its European Context*. Ed. E. Kooper. Cambridge Studies in Medieval Literature, 21. Cambridge: Cambridge University Press, 1994. Pages 96–112.

Bevington, David. *Medieval Drama*. Boston: Houghton Mifflin, 1975.

Boase, Roger. *The Origin and Meaning of Courtly Love: A Critical Study of European Scholarship*. Manchester: University of Manchester Press, 1977.

Bradley, Ritamary. "Backgrounds of the Title *Speculum* in Mediaeval Literature." *Speculum* 29 (1954): 100–115.

Busby, Keith, and Erik Kooper, eds. *Courtly Literature: Culture and Context*. Utrecht Publications in General and Comparative Literature, 25. Amsterdam and Philadelphia: J. Benjamins, 1990.

Campbell, L. "The Art Market in the Southern Netherlands in the Fifteenth Century." *The Burlington Magazine* 118, 2 (April 1976): 188–98.

Coupe, W. A. "Ungleiche Liebe: A Sixteenth Century Topos." *Modern Language Review* 62 (1967): 661–71.

Davis, N. Zemon. "Women on Top: Symbolic Sexual Inversion and Political Disorder in Early Modern Europe." *The Reversible World*. Ed. Barbara A. Babcock. Ithaca: Cornell University Press, 1978. Pages 147–90.

Decker, Therese. "*Lanseloet van Denemerken* and its biblical source." *Canadian Journal of Netherlandic Studies* 8 (1987–88): 12–27.

Deschamps, J. *Middelnederlandse Handschriften uit Europese en Amerikaanse Bibliotheken: Catalogus*. Brussels: Koninklijke Zuidnederlandse Maatschappij voor Taal- en Letterkunde en Geschiedenis, 1970.

Dijk, H. van. "Als ons die Astrominen Lesen: Over het Abel Spel *Vanden Winter ende vanden Somer.*" *Tussentijds: Bundel Studies Aangeboden aan W. P. Gerritsen ter Gelegenheid van zijn Vijftigste Verjaardag.* Ed. A. M. J. van Buuren et al. Utrecht: HES, 1985. Pages 56–70.

———. "The Drama Texts in the Van Hulthem Manuscript." *Medieval Dutch Literature in the European Context.* Ed. Erik Kooper. Cambridge Studies in Medieval Literature, 21. Cambridge University Press, 1994. Pages 283–96.

———. "De Graaf van Blois Bezoekt een Zoldertheater in Dordrecht." *Nederlandse Literatuur, een Geschiedenis.* Ed. M. A. Schenkeveld-van der Dussen et al. Groningen: Nijhoff, 1993. Pages 62–67.

———. "*Lanseloet van Denemerken*: One of the *Abele Spelen* in the Hulthem Ms." *Popular Drama in Northern Europe in the Later Middle Ages: A Symposium.* Ed. Fleming G. Andersen et al. Odensee University Press, 1988. Pages 101–12.

———. "The Structure of the 'Sotternieën' in the Hulthem Manuscript." *The Theatre in the Middle Ages.* Ed. H. Braet, J. Nowé, and G. Tournoy. Leuven: Leuven University Press, 1985. Pages 238–50.

Dijk, H. van, W. P. Gerritsen, Orlanda S. H. Lie, and F. Van der Poel, eds. *Klein Kapitaal uit het Handschrift Van Hulthem.* Hilversum: Verloren, 1992.

Dirk of Delft. *Tafel vanden Kersten Ghelove.* Ed. Father L. M. Daniëls, O.P. Antwerp: Ons Geestelijk Erf Publications, 1937–39. 4 volumes.

Duinhoven, A. M., "Boerenbedrog in *Die buskenblaser.*" *De Nieuwe Taalgids* 87 (1994): 195–203.

———. "De Bron van *Esmoreit*" *De Nieuwe Taalgids* 72 (1979): 124–44.

———. "De Bron van *Lanseloet.*" *Tijdschrift voor Nederlandse Taal- en Letterkunde* 95 (1979): 262–87.

———. "Corruptie is Overal." *De Nieuwe Taalgids* 70 (1977): 97–120.

———. "De Epilogen van *Die Buskenblaser, Esmoreit, en Truwanten.*" *Opstellen door Vrienden en Vakgenoten Aangeboden aan Dr. C. H. A. Kruyskamp.* Ed. Hans Heestermans. 's-Gravenhage: M. Nijhoff, 1977. Pages 63–77.

———. "Mere van den Lanseloet." *Tijdschrift voor Nederlandse Taal- en Letterkunde* 96 (1980): 12–16.

———. "Over Gloriant van Brunswijc en Florentine van Abelant." *Wie Veel Leest Heeft Veel te Verantwoorden . . . F. Lulofs.* Groningen: RU Nederlands Instituut, 1980. Pages 81–99.

———. "Pleidooi voor Reconstructie van *Esmoreit.*" *Spiegel der Letteren* 17 (1975): 241–67.

———. "Tekstreconstructie een Abel Spel." *Spiegel der Letteren* 19 (1977): 193–244.

————. "Van Moses tot Esmoreit." *Spektator* 10 (1980–81): 566–76.

Edwards, Robert R., and Stephen Spector, eds. *The Olde Daunce: Love, Friendship, Sex, and Marriage in the Medieval World* Albany: State University of New York Press, 1991.

Es, G. A. van. "Het Negeren van Tijd en Afstand in de Abele Spelen." *Tijdschrift voor Nederlandse Taal- en Letterkunde* 73 (1955): 161–92.

Flanigan, C. Clifford. "Comparative Literature and the Study of Medieval Drama," *Yearbook of Comparative and General Literature* 35 (1986): 56–104.

Gibson, Walter S. *Breugel.* New York: Thames and Hudson, 1993.

Gilbert, Martin. *British History Atlas.* London: Weidenfeld and Nicolson, 1968.

Gravdal, K. *Ravishing Maidens: Writing Rape in Medieval French Literature and Law.* Philadelphia: University of Pennsylvania Press, 1991.

————. *Vilain and Courtois: Transgressive Parody in French Literature of the Twelfth and Thirteenth Centuries.* Lincoln, Neb., and London: University of Nebraska Press, 1989.

Greetham, David C. *Textual Scholarship: An Introduction.* New York and London: Garland, 1992.

Hoogenbeemt, Roza van. "De Voorstelling van de Gekruisigde van de XIIe tot de XVIIe Eeuw." *Ons Geestelijk Erf* 22 (1948): 201–36.

Hummelen, W. M. H. "Performers and Performance in the Earliest Serious Secular Plays in the Netherlands." *Comparative Drama* 26 (1992): 19–33.

————. "Tekst en Toneelinrichting in de Abele Spelen." *De Nieuwe Taalgids* 70 (1977): 229–42.

Iwema, K. "Beschouwingen over de *Gloriant*." *Spiegel der Letteren* 7 (1964): 241–52.

————. "Waer Sidi—over een Middelnederlandse Toneel-conventie." *De Nieuwe Taalgids* 77 (1984): 48–61.

————. "De Wereld van een Abel Spel: *Vanden Winter ende vanden Somer* Herbeschouwd." *De Nieuwe Taalgids* 80 (1987): 21–27.

Jente, Richard, ed. *Proverbia Communia: A Fifteenth Century Collection of Dutch Proverbs with the Low German Version.* Indiana University Publications Folklore Series, 4. Bloomington: Indiana University Press, 1947.

Johnson, David F., ed. and trans. *Penninc and Pieter Vostaert: Roman van Walewein.* New York and London: Garland Publishing, 1992.

Jonckbloet, W. J. A. *Geschiedenis van de Middelnederlandsche Dichtkunst.* Amsterdam: P.N. van Kampen, 1851–55. 3 Volumes.

Kazemier, G. "De Bron van Lanseloet?" *Tijdschrift voor Nederlandse Taal- en Letterkunde* 96 (1980): 1–11.

————. "Lanseloet van Denemerken." *Taal- en Letterkundig Gastenboek voor Professor Dr. G. A. van Es.* Groningen: Archief voor de Nederlandse Syntaxis, 1975. Pages 229–36.

Koekman, Jeannette. "De Stilte rond Sanderijn: Over het Abel Spel *Lanseloet van Denemerken.*" *De Canon onder Vuur.* Ed. E. van Alphen and Maaike Meijer. Amsterdam: Van Gennep, 1991. Pages 20–34.

Kooper, Erik, ed. *Medieval Dutch Literature in its European Context.* Cambridge Studies in Medieval Literature, 21. Cambridge: Cambridge University Press, 1994.

Kuiper, Willem. "Van *Averne* naar *Denemerken*; Waarheen en Hoe Ver?" Spiegel der Letteren 39 (1997): 291–97.

Lerner, Robert E. "Vagabonds and Little Women: The Medieval Netherlandish Dramatic Fragment *De Truwanten.*" *Modern Philology* 65 (May 1968): 301–06.

Lewis, C. B. "The Origins of the Weaving Songs and the Theme of the Girl at the Fountain." *PMLA* 37, 2 (1922): 141–81.

Lie, Orlanda S. H. "Het Abel Spel van Lanseloet van Denemerken in het Handschrift-Van Hulthem: Hoofse Tekst of Stadsliteratuur?" *Op Belofte van Profijt.* Ed. H. Pleij. Amsterdam: Prometheus, 1991. Pages 200–16.

———. "*Die Hexe* in het Perspectief van Middelnederlandse Toverboeken." *Madoc* 4 (1990): 212–20.

Liungman, Waldemar. *Der Kampf zwischen Sommer und Winter.* FF Communications 130. Helsinki: Academia Scientiarum Fennica, 1941.

Meurs, Frank van. "De Abele Spelen en de Navolgende Sotternieën als Thematisch Tweeluik." *Literatuur,* 5, 3 (1988): 149–56.

Mierlo, J. van. "Het Dramatisch Conflict in Lanseloet van Denemerken." *Verslagen en Mededelingen van de Koninklijke Vlaamsche Academie voor Taal- en Letterkunde,* 1942. Pages 339–57.

Newman, F. X., ed. *The Meaning of Courtly Love.* Albany: State University of New York Press, 1968.

Nicholas, David. *Domestic Life of a Medieval City: Women, Children and the Family in Fourteenth Century Ghent.* Lincoln: University of Nebraska Press, 1985.

Olivier, L. J. J. "Pleidooi voor Damiet." *Tijdschrift voor Nederlandse Taal- en Letterkunde* 65 (1947): 174–80.

Olsen, Michel. "Miracles de Nostre Dame par Personnages." *Popular Drama in Northern Europe in the Later Middle Ages: A Symposium.* Ed. Flemming G. Andersen et al. Odensee University Press, 1988. Pages 41–63.

Oostrom, Frits Pieter van. *Court and Culture: Dutch Literature 1350–1450.* Trans. Arnold J. Pomerans. Berkeley: University of California Press, 1992.

Paepe, N. de. "Kunnen onze Beatrijslegende en Abele Spelen Geëvalueerd Worden door Middel van Andreas Capellanus' De Arte Honeste Amandi?" *Leuvense Bijdragen* 53 (1964): 120–47.

Peeters, L. "Esmoreit in het Geding." *Spiegel der Letteren* 20 (1978): 266–72.

_____. *"Esmoreit Tconincx Sone van Cecielien*: Siciliaanse Historie als Abel Spel." *Spiegel der Letteren* 19 (1977): 245–79.

Peteri, B. H. "Over Esmoreit." *Tijdschrift voor Nederlandse Taal- en Letterkunde* 64 (1946): 3–28.

Pleij, Herman. "Hoe Interpreteer je een Middelnederlandse Tekst?" *Spektator* 6 (1976–77): 337–49.

_____. "De Laatmiddeleeuwse Rederijkersliteratuur als Vroeg-humanistische Overtuigingskunst." *Jaarboek der Koninklijke Souvereine Kamer van Rhetorica van Vlaanderen de Fonteijne* 34 (1984): 65–95.

_____. *Het Literaire Leven in de Middeleeuwen.* 2nd, revised edition. Leiden: M. Nijhoff, 1988.

_____, ed. *Op Belofte van Profijt: Stadsliteratuur en Burgermoraal in de Nederlandse Letterkunde van de Middeleeuwen.* Amsterdam: Prometheus, 1991.

_____. "Over de Betekenis van Middelnederlandse Teksten." *Spektator* 10 (1980–81): 299–339.

_____. "The Rise of Urban Literature in the Low Countries." *Medieval Dutch Literature in the European Context.* Ed. Erik Kooper. Cambridge Studies in Medieval Literature, 21. Cambridge University Press, 1994. Pages 62–77.

_____. *De Sneeuwpoppen van 1511: Stadscultuur in de Late Middeleeuwen.* Amsterdam: Meulenhoff, 1988.

_____. "De Sociale Funktie van Humor en Trivialiteit op het Rederijkerstoneel." *Spektator* 5 (1975–76): 108–27.

_____. "Volksfeest en Toneel in de Middeleeuwen I, II." *Revisor* 3 (1976): 52–63, and *Revisor* 4 (1977): 34–41.

Plummer, John F. "The Woman's Song in Middle English and Its European Backgrounds." *Vox Feminae.* Ed. John Plummer. Kalamazoo: Medieval Institute Publications, 1981. Pages 135–54.

Ramondt, Marie. "Van Jaarspel tot Abel Spel." *De Gids* 106, 4 (1942–44): 165–84.

Réau, Louis. *Iconographie de l'art chrétien.* Paris: Presses Universitaires de France, 1955–59. 6 Parts in 3 Volumes.

Reed, Thomas L., Jr. *Middle English Debate Poetry and the Aesthetics of Irresolution.* Columbia: University of Missouri Press, 1990.

Schlauch, Margaret. *Chaucer's Constance and Accused Queens.* 1927. Rpt. New York: Gordian Press, 1969.

Schotter, Anne Howland. "Woman's Song in Medieval Latin." *Vox Feminae.* Ed. John F. Plummer. Kalamazoo: Medieval Institute Publications, 1981. Pages 19–33.

Serrure, C. P. "Het Groot Hulthemsch Handschrift." *Vaderlandsch Museum.* Gent: Hoste, 1859–60. Vol. III, 139–64.

Simon, Eckehard, ed. *The Theatre of Medieval Europe: New Research in Early Drama.* Cambridge Studies in Medieval Literature, 9. Cambridge: Cambridge University Press, 1991.

Sivirsky, A. L. I. "De Stamboom van Esmoreit." *Spiegel der Letteren* 20 (1978): 257–65.

Sondergaard, Leif, and Thomas Pettitt. "The Flyting of Yule and Lent." *The Early Drama, Art, and Music Review* 16 (1993): 1–11.

Steketee, C. J. H. "Rawast in Afrijka." *Nieuwe Taalgids* 50 (1957): 330.

Stewart, Alison. *Unequal Lovers: A Study of Unequal Couples in Northern Art.* New York: Abaris, 1978.

Strietman, Elsa. "The Low Countries." *The Theatre of Medieval Europe.* Ed. Eckehard Simon. Cambridge: Cambridge University Press, 1991. Pages 225–52.

Stuiveling, Garmt. "De Structuur van de Abele Spelen." *Vakwerk: Twaalf Studies in Literatuur.* Zwolle: Tjeenk Willink, 1967. Pages 7–43.

Traver, Hope. "Religious Implications in the *Abele-Spelen* of the Hulthem Manuscript." *The Germanic Review* 26 (1951): 34–49.

Uhland, L. "Sommer und Winter." *Schriften zur Geschichte der Dichtung und Sage.* Stuttgart: Gotta, 1866. Vol. III, 17–51.

Vanhamme, M. *Bruxelles: de Bourg Rural à Cité Mondiale.* Anvers/Bruxelles: Mercurius, 1968.

Waddel, Helen. *Mediaeval Latin Lyrics.* London: Constable; New York: Barnes and Noble, 1966.

Waerden, Kees van der. "De Figuur van de Cockijn in het Abel Spel *Vanden Winter ende vanden Somer.*" *Spektator* 15 (1985–86): 268–77.

Walther, H. *Das Streitgedicht in der lateinische Literatur des Mittelalters.* München: Beck, 1920.

Welter, J. Th., ed. *Tabula Exemplorum secundum Ordinem Alphabeti: Receuil d'Exempla Compilé en France à la Fin du xiiie Siècle.* 1927. Rpt. Geneve: Slatkine, 1973.

Wijngaards, N. C. H. "Andreas Capellanus' *De Arte Honeste Amandi* en de Abele Spelen." *Spiegel der Letteren* 5 (1961): 218–28.

———. "De Oorsprong der Abele Spelen en Sotternieën." *Handelingen der Koninklijke Zuidnederlandse Maatschappij voor Taal- en Letterkunde en Geschiedenis* 22 (1968): 411–23.

———. "Structuurvergelijking bij de Abele Spelen." *Levende Talen* 215 (1962): 322–27.

Worp, J. A. *Geschiedenis van het Drama en van het Tooneel in Nederland.* 1904. Rpt. Rotterdam: Langeveld, 1970. Vol. I.